HONORING OUR CREATOR

By Honoring our Inner "small" Voice
to Honor Our Common "Daddy"

LINK THOMPSON

Ordering Information:

Books to Life Marketing Ltd
70 Coulson's Road, Bristol BS14 0NW, UK

Printed in the United States of America

Worldwide hashtags links:

#OurCreator

#OurCommonDaddy?

#WhosyourDaddy?

#WhosOurDaddy?

#whosourdaddy?

Search engine keyword: Creator

This book is dedicated to the Donkey for its long overdue recognition of loyal servant service to Our Creator, as a subtle; yet created as a visual authenticator of His Word!!!

Acknowledgements and Appreciations

To my Uncle Elwood and my Sweetheart's Mother, Mom Evelyn for their tireless, guiding spiritual light for their family members and many others.

To Pastor Joel Osteen for his inspiring messages that often trigger my "pen" to reveal my internalized appreciation of Our Amazing, Totally Awesome Creator Father!!!

Contents

Preface

This book is about Choice. Our Creator gave us two choices: Go Positive, or go negative. If you choose negative, never mind reading this book until you sense an inner voice "spirit" itch. Just know, going negative is a rejection of Our Positive Natured Creator and unpardonable.

Just know that Our Creator sees all his kids as Positive Blessings. Thus, like any true Father; especially Our Common "Daddy," Our Positive Natured Creator forgives in a split second, then forgets. So, if now curious enough, say in the size of a "mustard seed," read on and then follow the trail of the Donkey!!!

NOTE

I WILL BE CAPITALIZING ANYTHING AND EVERYTHING ABOUT OUR CREATOR IN my BOOK TO DISTINCTIVLY HONOR OUR CREATOR'S DEITY AND HIS WORD. WITH LOYAL AND TREASURED RESPECT, I WILL IN BE VIOLATING EVERYDAY GRAMMAR RULES, AND NOT CAPTILIZING THE WORD "my" THROUGHOUT THIS MEMOIR.

my CREATOR'S COMMISSION

Written in 2015 as my About for a lengthy Word Press website profile of me, my quest and my commission to Honor Our Creator Father and His Son, Jesus:

"Who's Our Daddy?" An ageless, rhetorical question that we probably all ponder during our lives. I contend that each of us is born with an inherited awareness of a Supreme Being, or Our Creator. Each of us is created as unique individuals: yet, we all bleed red and with interchangeable parts. So, let us forget race and let us focus on that internal itch within our person or soul, to find and define our common Creator "Daddy."

We were created with the power of choice and in my opinion, choice is a prerequisite in finding Our Creator Spiritually. Choice provides mankind the power to either accept our spirit itch as Our Creator Spiritually communicating with us, or reject. Choice provides mankind the opportunity to measure Our

Creator's Spiritual Good, in terms of Grace and Love, against the opposite. These moments of spiritual struggle can and has since the beginning of mankind, had the causal impact of numerous interpretations; often leading to religions. These religions can be readily researched in Wikipedia and probably evolved for survival and social needs as well. To blindly follow a trending religion, an individual may run the risk of distractions and distortions, and then miss a nirvana relationship with our "one" true Creator. Thus, it becomes vital to correlate, or connect any religion to the Creator Himself!

Hello, my first name is Link and I kept my last name anonymous, while I developed my 2015 website, and conducted a worldwide cyber-outreach, teaser-blogging discussions to generate an impending eBook. my mission was, and still is, to collect and culminate worldwide thoughts and opinions regarding Our Common Creator Daddy. And above all, always Honoring Our Creator!!! Thus, the title of my book, and I use three exclamations points to Honor the Trinity as well.

Which since led to this impending hardcover book as well, by Link Thompson, soon to be published. And now this "About" opens the door to my continued quest to Honor Our Creator Father as Our Common Daddy. This question as to "Who's Our Daddy," has intrigued mankind since the beginning of thoughtful soul searching. Thus, the seeking and finding a common, worldwide understanding of who Our Creator "is," and becomes the singular premise for my website and this author's blogging. This author's wish is that my website forum will respectfully enlighten all visitors; hopefully, from worldwide replies that are informative, regardless if one agrees, or disagrees. All replies should be civil as my website forum is meant to honor and to hear Our Creator's Voice through mutual soul sharing. This forum will be kept both theology lite and science lite as well.

Theology lite because there are countless religions stemming from the beginning of mankind's arrival on our incredible planet Earth. No personal beliefs, or religions will be critiqued, evaluated, or judged on my website. That is a personal choice given by Our Creator!!! After traveling most of our wonderful world, it is this author's observation, that religions evolved from the ageless, internal question of who is Our Daddy, and the natural desire to be individually, or collectively respectful to their perceived Deity. However, there are also religions; that in essence, are a rejection. So, my website outreach question continues, "which are you?"

my website and blog will also be kept science lite. From Wikipedia research, noted scientists and philosophers, understandably leaned toward the laws of nature and/or pantheism. While not to be interpreted as a religion in itself, this author is fully in concert with monotheism and one Creator. Why you ask? As a retired military fighter pilot and a retired commercial airline pilot; and to include the consensus from post mission quotes by our famed astronauts: We aviators conclude, by sight, that Our Creator is Alive and Well, End of Story!!! But "Who is He?" And "How does He do His thing?"

Scientists and philosophers generally earn their credentials within confined surroundings. However, Our Creator's Majesty as viewed by our astronauts from the moon, or space travel itself, is surely an equal, reputable surrounding to conclude that Our Creator lives. This author's forty-five years of aviation, included numerous hours of soul-searching time and enjoying Our Creator's priceless views from around thirty-five thousand feet, while flying to several worldwide destinations. The awesome majesty of our world was later appreciated on an around-the-world ocean cruise as well; yet, Our Creator's Majesty can be readily witnessed in a newborn baby, a newborn animal, a blossoming flower, or a cut on your finger that heals itself.

Like scientists and philosophers before me, I have no conflict with their alignment around the laws of nature, or any other means from the beginnings of scientific assessments. All can be respected as a personalized, intuitive correlation toward an explainable Deity; however, in my Opinion, it is a step short. Like our famed astronauts, it also becomes intuitive, by sight or "seeing is believing," that Our "Invisible Spirit" Creator should be our first response and answer to: "Who's Our Daddy?" When we research the many religions, the reference to "in the beginning" is used, but leaving cerebral room for personal interpretations about the "event" itself.

Aviators by profession, become energy conscious and knowledgeable by necessity. Numerous flight hours around thirty-five thousand feet is an excellent place to connect the dots about the full realm of energy and its Laws. And up there with clear skies and clear thinking, I began to connect Our Creator's Words "In the Beginning" to a massive "energy event." Nothing could have occurred without involving "energy." The word energy appears to have evolved with Aristotle (384-322BC); yet, not connected to the "In the Beginning" event by theologians; nor scientists as clearly as I would have expected by now. They were content then, and still are to this day, with their separate twists that seem to align by definition with Deism.

The Laws of Energy would explain the resultant Laws of Nature on our mother earth and all other Universe phenomenon as the Hand of Our Creator running the show.

When one considers the magnitude of everything that we now know about our creation: Is it a stretch to think of Our Creator in terms of Energy; and more specifically, in terms of "Spiritual" Energy as well? Is it a stretch to think of Our Creator as a Spiritual Mastermind, capable of controlling all forms of transmutable energy, that respond collectively, or singular, within the Laws of Conservation of Energy. These laws state that energy is neither gained, nor lost, are well known by mankind and are seemingly implicit when we corelate our internal spiritual itch to Our Awesome Daddy. Seemingly implicit is that all things become possible through Our Creator, either tangible or intangible, visible or invisible.

The "intangible" or "invisible" part of the "Creator equation," is where we can connect our "personal itch" to find Our Daddy by Honoring Our Inner "small" Voice.

In contrast to Deism, we have Theism where Our Creator is available 24/7 to mingle among His creation and responds to Faith that He can sense spiritually via our Inner "small" Voice. This author contends that both Faith and Love have energy-like qualities. Both Faith and Love have powerful Positive impacts for anyone that connects with Our Creator. A nirvana relationship with Our Creator in terms of Faith and Love, should not be construed as another religion. This author contends that both are an innate, instinctive personal gift from Our Creator, to find Him by choice, on our personal time table; or, during a time of needed Grace, as another anytime gift from Our Creator Father.

For this author, thinking of Our Creator in terms of Energy, instantly clarified the mystery of "In the Beginning" and "Who my Daddy Is." Or, all that I can see and all that I cannot see. Plus, through Our Creator's "Spiritual Energy" connecting with our personal "Faith Energy," it clarified and also completes the pathway of Life, from the Creator and back to the Creator upon our passing. This author contends that the only way to lose this spiritual energy pathway to the Creator is to "openly reject" the Creator's Deity, and sadly, the trailing essence within the definition of Deism. The Gospel's clarity regarding the unpardonable sin, is in concert with the Gospel caveats; thus, protecting thereafter the return pathway for the innocent, the unknowing, and most assuredly, include unborn babies, whom are also recorded in the Creator's Book of Life. Do not think of this relationship as a religion, but rather straight talk, connecting the dots in terms of explainable energy logic within our Universe. More specifically, in terms of Spiritual Energy as our pathway connection to Our Awesome Common Daddy, from our birth to our return. Just say "Please" and that is enough "Positive" Energy Faith, the size of a "mustard seed," to grant your wish as guaranteed by Our Creator Father's Word, and of course, my Hero, Jesus!!! Since Our Creator Daddy gave His kids the power of choice, we can also reject, and then live, die and re-assimilate into our earthly "digs." But like any loving Father, the good news is that we and all vacillators, or rejectors can always change our minds anytime, anyplace by just repeating, or just paraphrasing John 3:16. Jesus covered all situations on the Cross; then so stated in His final words and recorded for all time in John 19:30.

In the energy realm, any Positive "belief" energy flow is enough faith energy for Our Creator Daddy to grant your wish to be included in His pathway return into eternal spiritual life. Additionally, I fully believe that all who have never heard of Our Creator; thus, never rejected their Creator Father will surely be included as well. What Father; especially, a "Creator" Father would forget His Unborn, all His Babies, His mentally disabled, the similarly inflicted, or even the conflicted, who seek with only the belief of a "mustard seed," etc.; thus, "all," in my Opinion, will surely be autosaved into eternal life. Since no negative wrongs were committed, case closed!!! Only religions delineate and measure; so, for the able minded who choose by choice to Honor their Inner "small" Voices; then, if "No" rejection, "No" works required, just Faith, and everlasting Trust fulfills John 19:30!!! Any other conclusion would devalue the horrific price paid by my Personal Hero, Jesus!!!

In my about, I stated that I would one day write a book, so here goes: Some of my enjoyable Blessings have been Broadway plays, so I will present my life storyline in scenes. The "Lion King," a definite favorite of mine, comes to mind as a comparable light-hearted storyline filled with my inner "small" voice enlightenments; within a wisdom-growing format—my youth till the present. Starting advice before pulling the curtain on soon to be 80 years, always make your bed "in the morning!" That simple Positive daily step and/or mindset, is also in-step with Our Positive Creator Daddy, and will have mysterious, popup trailing Blessings!!! This book is full of such Blessings!!!

SCENE

I

my "in the beginning"

It's quite safe to say that just about everything that comes to mind, starts with the scribed thought, "in the beginning." my "in the beginning," written as a reader-teaser to HONOR OUR CREATOR, sets my lifelong stage for my tribute to Honor HIS "IN THE BEGINNING." And so is the goal of my blog-a-book and/or hard cover venture. my opening scene and associated storyline began during my stick-horse age era. And I might add upfront, it was the fastest stick horse around, so fast that somewhere on that open range in northwest North Dakota, a "bag of pennies" fell out of my "saddle bag" pockets. So, who do you call? Especially, when you are out in a cow pasture. By that age, I had already been spanked for carrying matches around the farm, so smoke signals were out and only our local Assiniboine Native Americans would understand smoke texting.

Their teepee locations near spring-fed sloughs are still discernible by rings of rocks and like New York City, this North Dakota range area now has a crazy address like the corner of 98th Street Northwest and 134th Avenue Northwest. You will have found the area when you see a rock house that looks like a fort. And you will also be looking at the free land given to my Grandparents, once they reached North Dakota after immigrating from Norway. Both my Grandparents and my Parents gave survival-like farming their all and are now also interred nearby. That setting sort of sets the timeline, no cell phones; nor electricity until I was around five or six.

Well, I called on "God" to help me find my saved fortune of pennies. I had been to summer Bible school by this age; so, I knew just enough about "GOD," to know that He knew everything. And probably through His eyes, knew exactly where my lost bag of pennies was in our cow pasture. Bible school teachers taught kid-friendly Positive virtues; but by then, I also had been told that "God" knew if we were good or "bad". The traveling pastors were quick to use the "fear" word in their messages, and I never did find my lost bag of pennies. Thus, my walk-away impression of "GOD," became confusing and lasted far too long. What a horrible thing to do to a child. However, I was Blessed to have an Uncle with a lily-white soul, who married my Dad's sister, and her name was Lillie. And by his example, steered me in the direction of Positive respect of my inner "small" voice. And that Our Creator Father, from the onset of His "IN THE BEGINNING," is and would always be talking directly to me. "Siri" and I will continue enlightening my book cover tagline that Honors Our Creator's means of "Spiritually Talking" to His mankind creation via our inner "small" voice.

Uncle Elwood led by example, which I cannot repeat enough, and cleverly used Our Creator's mountain lake environment up in British Columbia to set the stage for "what's not to love about Our Creator!" So much to enjoy that British Columbia would later become a favorite family trout fishing vacation for my Sweetheart and my two Super Sons Yup! All unforeseen Blessings!!! Who could have or would have guessed that this stick horse cowboy, 55 years later, would also lease and captain forty-foot trawlers around the nearby San Juan Islands and Victoria Island. And all aboard would just melt with appreciation of the Orca Whales who would occasionally surround the boat, check us out, give us the eye, give us camera shots and welcome us to the area.

Our Creator Father deals only in Positives, such as Faith, Hope and the greatest of all, Love! Fear teachings are negatives and will be treated as such in this book. Fear teachings are an earthly thing meant to stir the rejectors, or the all night partiers and the church front row absentees. Thus, I moved on to life observations and awareness that our Creator is quite the opposite of fear and negatives. So did Job, and per the oldest book in Our Creator's Word, I rest my faith in Job 34:10. my conclusions are that Our Creator can "only" do Positives, or things associated with Goodness and Grace, AMEN!!!

Such things as earthquakes, fires, hurricanes, and tornadoes are often associated with Our Creator's negative side, but in reality, are tied to the laws of nature as a result of our creation. What "Creator" by definition, would deal in negatives such as fear, or harm His Creation. The only negative I had was that I never did find my pennies, but since, the "God" of my youth; now my Creator Father, has since Blessed this North Dakota farm boy "well" beyond my wildest dreams and expectations. Yup!!! my Creator "Daddy" was listening all along!!! And apparently, I had been sufficiently listening to my inner "small" voice as well!!! "Siri" found these comments by Doctor Gail Brenner that really chimed in with my life: "The true path for our lives cannot be figured out or created. Our job is simply to listen, and in the listening, we will be given all the guidance we need, to do exactly the right thing. When we listen, life unfolds mysteriously, we get out of our own way and allow the "still, small" voice to be Heard."

Looking back, I always had just enough and was Blessed "not" so much in "pennies" or entrapped mentally in money wealth, but in Blessings where I got to appreciate and enjoy Our Creator's Majesty. As I compose this hard cover book and/or blog-a-book for my website endeavor, I must include first, my Awesome Creator Blessings of the births of my two Sons, their Mom, my eventual Daughter by marriage, my three Grandchildren, my twenty-seven nieces and nephews, their parents, my adopted European family, and never least, my numerous fellow Air Force aviators and brother-like compadres. Plus, memories of nearly everywhere on our mother earth, except the Antarctica. The good news is that our refrigerator came with an ice maker. So, I will let that go and watch it on National Geographic channels. However, I have flown over its cousin, the Artic, and Greenland several times. And for the record, I grew up in North Dakota and that should count as a trip to either artic region. Actually, I have hard evidence of the Ice Age, I found a "hard" rock with fossilized sea shells on our farm. It's now a door stop in our Florida home, and next to it, is an axeblade shaped piece of mining shale from a Lake Ta-Weel fish camp in British Columbia. This perfect shaped door stop is a perfect reminder of bucket loads of Blessings that started with my Uncle Elwood. The mountain-unique lake trout fishing experiences were always enjoyed by my family and were also shared with our Floridian family-like friends; again, Blessings and memories never to be forgotten.

So, let's venture on and establish chronologically my credibility to humbly declare that Honoring Our Creator is NOT a religion, nor NEED to be a religion. The word religion is a mixed bag; and as employed or engaged around our global earth, much too often an embarrassment for me when I stand before Our Creator Father. And most certainly, an obstacle for Our Common Daddy to deal with. In my opinion, the issues among religions became a byproduct of the "Tower of Babel" event, as recorded in Our Creator's "In the Beginning", Genesis Chapter Eleven. This event has babbled or confused me for years, and most biblical scholars interpret this event as displeasing to Our Creator. In my bible school summer school years, my thoughts that a tower tribute up to "God's" Heaven was cool and a good thing, but not so. Our Creator is not into idolatry of any kind. In fact, He prefers to be closer to your Heart than your shirt pocket. my take is, that it may have been a natural communal occurrence to stir leadership, reduce habitat dependency and/ or overcrowding, and eventually resulted into subtle language differences. Different strokes for different peoples led to different languages and different interpretations, and still a tossup issue around the globe as I write this book.

Naïve, but full of eagle-like curiosity and vinegar to discover the unknown, my farm-boy taught manners opened lots of new doors. I entered the University of Oregon at the age of seventeen and not mature enough, nor cool enough to compete with kids from California. Got a big fat "F" minus on my first English composition paper; so, I hope my publisher will get me a passing grade on this "book" composition.

Looking back, not sure how I qualified for the University of Oregon. Nothing in my high school education prepped me for that SAT experience. No book stores with prep books, nor courses available in NW North Dakota, so I took it cold. So naïve, that I did not even know how to guess right. But, by the Grace of the Dean of Our Creation, I got accepted to the University of Donald Duck. I did well in my major, but not so good in Greek literature. However, I could spell Phi Kappa Sigma, as a new frat pledge. my lasting memory of attending the famed home for Olympic tryouts, or Hayward Field, is that I ran a four minute, ten second mile as a result of pacing with class mates, and occasionally, with two-time Olympic finalist, my class mate, Dyrol Burleson. Dyrol would honor the presence of all his fans for about three quarters of a mile, then step on the gas and cross the finish line around three minutes and fifty-five seconds. What a show off, but he was exactly one-year older than I, so probably more practice.

Eventually, I became overwhelmed by mounting college costs and its impact on my parents. I sort of knew that my days were numbered, but pressed on, always looking for a pony in my life bag of smelly challenges. my Dad only attended school through the eighth grade and my Mom through high school, so looking homeward only meant farm work. No thanks! So initially, I earned spending money working for the University library in their film and sound department. That position got me into sound setups and management for University events; such as, the Kingston Trio performance at the basketball arena. I always loved their song, the "Sloop John B." Little did I know that one day, I would actually own a sloop, the "Nurse T & Skipper Me," and sail it from Florida to Maine. Yup, what an unforeseen Blessing!!!

With tastes and yearnings to be as cool as the kids from California, I attempted to make up the difference by cleaning restaurants after closing and other part time jobs. I added enough to even afford my first car, a 1955 Pontiac Chieftain convertible—and since, three more convertibles and five sports cars—all fun Blessings. Now California cool, I was cool enough to enjoy a fun fraternity social life, close to where the movie "Animal House" was filmed later and when watching the movie, it was a noticeably familiar old house, both inside and outside. But due to my immaturity and ever shortage of funds, my study habits and grades began to slip. So, after a disappointing sophomore year, I returned to North Dakota to regroup. I found a job making good money working on an oil well, but blatantly dangerous with muddy and slippery working areas. And with heavy pipes and chain winches that would ruin your life in a flash. So, on a very cold day in December 1961; with twenty dollars in my pocket, I decided to join the Air Force for a warm bunk and three squares a day. Best move I ever made!!! And of course, later on, my other best move, marrying my Sweetheart, in February 1971; and about to celebrate our "Golden!!!" Thus, the course for this book is to enlighten my opening "Preface" and to compose my vision and/or version of Our Creator's Universe through the lens of Positives, Energy Perceptions and most of all, Blessings!!!

SCENE

II

my Air Force Era

The day a new recruit joins the military, the last thing on your mind is anything except survival and concern for the unknown. Fortunately for me, I had some Air Force ROTC training at the University of Oregon to cushion the situation. What I am saying is that except for applying my ROTC style points, I was not thinking about, nor Honoring Our Creator Father at the time. However, as time went on, or during my Air Force prelude, He had not forgotten me and He was surely thinking about me as my Blessings began to subtly occur and evolve. Yet, I did not think of them as such, until much later in life when I was flying internationally during my DC-10 and B-747 Airline Era. By nature of the job, pilots have lots of introspection time at an altitude of 35,000 feet. But habitually, first-class crew meals and small talk always came first; plus, the dinners were enjoyably served by fun loving, party-minded flight attendants. Recalling one young lady, probably young enough to be my daughter, would change the color of her contact lens on every flight; thus, love your job, Positive workplace spiritual enlightenments. And after landing, and abiding by common crew no waste policies, the head flight attendant would typically mix all the leftover, or open booze and wine into one big jug of hooch for the crew bus trip to the layover hotel.

It is rare for flights anywhere to be smooth as glass. Among typical distracting disturbances during the flights, were moments dodging equator thunderstorms and their assured bumps at night. But then, there were the rewards of observing incredible star constellations, and my most memorable and notable, was the viewing of Haley's Comet; plus, the nightly viewing of the Southern Cross like a sailor's aid. Daytime views are less notable, unless flying over mountain ranges; such as the Alps, the Andes. or Greenland and the Artic regions. Nevertheless, no way can you not bring Our Creator into your thoughts as you appreciate His obvious Majesty!!! And as Apollo Moon Walker, Astronaut Gene Cernan summarily concluded: "There are no atheists in outer space!"

With prior ROTC time, I pulled and opened the curtain on Scene II. I enlisted with the understanding that I would be heading straight to flight training after basic, but no cigar. The aforementioned Airline Era Blessings came after twenty-four years of Air Force Era "stepping stones." After basic training, I went straight to electronics training as I had maxed the aptitude test, which in itself turned out to be a Blessing for years to follow. The Air Force had changed the rules and required that all its pilots needed college degrees; thus, I needed that stepping stone. As I was so military immature, it turned out to be a sharpening-time Blessing as well. I eventually qualified for an Air Force scholarship-like program to the University of Oklahoma. Thus, another Blessing, and as I write this chapter or scene, both my two OU's are in the top ten football rankings. One school is "green" and yellow; the other is "red" and white, what a nice unexpected 2019 Christmas colors Blessing. And the most unexpected seasonal Blessing blossomed right before my eyes, a bowl game, and I got to take my two Super Grandsons to an OU playoff game. I will leave it to my readers to research which OU.

After my "red" OU graduation, I went straight to Officer Training; then onto Pilot Training. I had joined an aero club during my enlisted years and I had acquired my private license in a Piper Cub. Plus, my electronics training was also compatible to maintain flight simulators; thus, gave me access for some instrument awareness. All this became a priceless value as I flew through Air Force pilot training in more ways than one and received my first choice upon graduation.

▸▸ The Supersonic F-100

I chose the F-100 Super Sabre, the very first Air Force fully operational, supersonic fighter on the planet. It had its own idiosyncrasies and "it" taught me how to fly, but what an honor and pleasure to have been respectfully associated with the "HUN" era. my time in the HUN was truly a Fighter Pilot Blessing. Amen!!!

As you might expect, my mind was on my airplane, its unforgiving nature and its mission, a hundred percent of the time. It seemed that the only time, any of "we, the living" pilots took time to Honor Our Creator, was during memorials for our lost fellow pilots. Looking back, my Creator Father stuck with me from the moment we discussed my lost pennies; and thank goodness, as the F-100 was called the "widow maker" for its aviation evolutionary surprises and its mission of close air support for my fellow Army and Marine ground troops. Enemy radar-controlled Quad-23's took two of my classmates, never to be forgotten. As a time line, July 20. 1969, Astronauts Armstrong and Aldrin landed and walked on the moon as I was shaving in our 510th TFS, Buzzard hooch in Bien Hoa, Vietnam.

Returning home to US soil in November 1969; I was so looking forward to allowing my mind to slowly return back to a "new" normal and kids. But after some sweet homecoming days and moments, my college and flight training time "Love" changed the conversations to her needs; to go her own way as daily worries of combat fears had taken its toll on her. Our chosen career worlds were becoming a mismatch as well: She was into a world requiring laboratory microscopes; mine was fighter aircraft radarscopes and then fly away into the wild blue yonder. The paperwork said "irreconcilable." Say what? But with more legal power than a 1000lb bomb and as burning to my inner heart and soul as napalm. However, amidst her caring honeymoon-like grace, our situation, her reasoning, became totally understandable, and shortly thereafter, I sadly watched her board a flight back to her new career. Hopefully stem cell research, as she was as brilliant as she was cutely beautiful. She could easily be mistaken for her look alike twin and their similar personality, Actress Sandy Duncan. I was thankful for our past, which included nearly three years of dating and over five years of marriage. So, I gave her everything except my tooth brush and my new Japanese stereo—which is still functioning in our family den. Played a lot of loud Creedence Clearwater Revival to drown "old" into "new" thinking. Later, a perfect situation song, the "Dance," by Garth Brooks has been my best medicine for that life surprise punch.

If I had any combat PTSD, it quickly vanished with a smile of a drop-dead, stunningly beautiful Texas girl that I met shortly after becoming single again. After 254 combat missions, she seemed angelic; even incarnate, a perfect accolade for her and triggered by the fact that she also attended the nearby University of the Incarnate Word. Her lovely smile could make men fall like dominoes. Miss Texas, was definitely an "Eleven" on a scale of one to ten and with a personality full of Tupelo Honey, an incredible song by Van Morison. I will always be forever thankful for her sweet healthcare-like moments after both a year in Vietnam and a surprise divorce upon my return. But there was this "Pope" concern: Somewhat concerned and sensitive that Miss Texas might have religion-led conflict issues with my divorcee status and border-line age difference; thus, I nurtured our relationship as if she were a true "Angel" only for and of the moment. Another concern: Miss Texas was getting her degree in Hospital Management, which sounded like what the Nuns did in the hospital where I was born. She had a noticeably pure Soul as well and definitely reachable for a time-honored service to Our Creator. So, since "Her" Creator out-ranked me and since the ink was not yet dry on my "your-free-card" from Miss Louisiana, this Air Force supersonic flight instructor needed to keep his mind at Mach One, or in the game, and no mental time available for new life complications. Actually, I did not want to be free, I wanted a family and Miss Texas was a definite Keeper!!!

In Texas, you will eventually become a George Strait fan. He seems to have a song for every situation and his song lyrics become forever reminders—all mine are forever sweet, none bitter. Country songs and honkytonk settings can provide lots of thinking time and answer lots of issues; however, I always felt a little out-of-step doing the "Cotton-Eyed-Joe" in Texas. So, maybe this North Dakota Norwegian was not in-step with swift-minded, southern girls at the moment and probably, a little combat dull after a year in Vietnam.

Shortly thereafter and like another country song, I married her polar opposite, as in Betty and Veronica in the comic book series Archie; another Eleven, my sister's best friend. But predictably sweet Miss Texas, still stunning and still with the heart of an Angel, kindly hosted my sailing stop on the north end of the Chesapeake/Delaware canal during my summer voyage to Maine. She kindly took me to several interesting local places of notable interest, like the famed Amish area and their horse drawn carriages. The Heresy's Chocolate factory was the well-known area attraction, but also nearby, a wolf sanctuary, where she had her chance to throw me to the "wolves." She was devoutly active in volunteer animal care, which thoroughly defined her consistent angelic nature. About here, all you savvy readers are surely asking, how did I know that Miss Texas lived near my sailing stop in Delaware. Well, that all started in Newark, NJ, back in the early 1990's. Several Continental airline pilots, now United, had a crew pad in a local downtown hotel. Like in my fraternity days, we had a "house mom" and he bought a new UpToDate computer, which had the USA "white pages" installed. During some crew rest time, I thought it would be fun to see where all my old and past friends were, including previous girlfriends.

I presumed that all previous girlfriends would be married, but to shorten this story, Miss Texas, popped up in another Newark, in next door Delaware. She did not become a Nun, but she did conduct our refreshed friendship and my sailing stopover visit like a Nun. She did manage a Veterans Hospital where her innate, transparent Soul could shine in service to countless Veterans, and forever revered by any Veteran, as a fellow Veteran. Sorry readers, but that situation all seemed rather preordained as I do not believe in coincidences.

The marina on the C/D canal was entered from the Delaware Bay and a stone's throw by boat up the bay, is the town of New Castle. It was a totally unique experience, a cobble stone experience that sets the timeline age of its existence. With Miss Texas from the famed city of "The Alamo," now leading me around this totally historic town, that uniquely answered my daily quest for a one-of-a-kind Happy Hour experience and never to be forgotten. Yes, it was JESSOP'S! A historical building dating back to 1674 and with a tavern-style woodwork and old wood flooring; now noticeably worn with perceivable trails. Now captured with a happy hour flavor and sounds of the past; just perfect for other fun-loving people like me, Miss Texas and possibly like our country's forefathers, such as Adams and Jefferson. Plausibly, their getaway from their offices in nearby Philadelphia and from their mentally challenging efforts to compose our country forming documents. As we all know, these documents have stood the test of time. Our framers all get all A's for their well thought out, still smoothly functioning compositions, written on "old parchments." And they did not have Microsoft Word as do I.

These authors of our Constitution and the Declaration of Independence may even have stayed at another deceased author, William Penn's home, as his house was down the block. The floors in this house were still in great shape and bring to mind other historical, uniquely memory making, east-coast stops during my sailing era. To name a few from the Chesapeake/Delaware Canal area, such as nearby Lewes, Delaware and nearby Annapolis with all its 18th century structures. A fellow combat vet and close friend from the mountains of Colorado, joined me for some sea level fun. We found an abundance of history to appreciate and for starters, the Naval Academy that cranked up in the mid-1840's. And outside their gate, was the uniquely famous Annapolis boat show.

So many boats; so little time, but we did our best. And outside their marina area, was another perfect Happy Hour location and its walls built in the late 1700's. Fresh beer and old floors, who knows who walked here in these hallowed settings.

From Annapolis and out their famous harbor, we sailed under the highway 50 bridge and zig zagged up to Baltimore. The marina that we chose was near the city center and rich with Happy Hour fun places. One place that neither of us will ever forget, was not for the food or the sailor's grog, but for our server. This gorgeous young lady spoke perfect English, and working to put herself through a nearby medical school. And never to be forgotten, she was from Siberia, near to where the Chelyabinsk meteor hit in 2013. The underlying message for both of we-Air Force Fighter Pilot Vets, was that we-both had done a small part to bring down the Berlin Wall and gave her the freedom to the rest of the world. Thus, a happy toast with our server and to her future; plus, a feel-good Blessing for me.

Some places were so uniquely satisfying, that leaving was ultra-difficult; thus, I stayed a month in loveable Savannah, Georgia. So many small parks to sit and imagine the history that occurred in this city, even a park where President George Washington used during his visits. This time period was setting the stage for my Matthew 28 aspirations, so those park settings were probably as instrumentally leading to my action steps as they were for President Washington. Here, one of my fellow Air Force forever friends, and near twin, who had joined me in Florida, took his inspiring, imprinted Matthew 28 cup, and returned to Texas after sailing with me for nearly a month. But not to worry, "our" former T-38 era boss joined me in Savannah, and for the rest of this book, I will refer to him as Mr. Half-Cup. Yup, when offered coffee, his typical morning pour request.

Like all good things, there comes a time for a sailor's itch to wonder on to new ports and new Happy Hours. So, continuing northerly on the noticeably curving ICW, we found Daufuskie Island, and available only by boat. What an unexpected cocktail of history that island stop turned out to be. However, still bugging me to this day, I accidentally left my forever precious, treasured Dad's cup on this island. This super special cup was given to me by eldest Son back when he was around twelve, and from his own hard-earned money. I expect that my Dad's cup is now being used in the marina super casual, family-style restaurant after being found next to an Adirondack chair near the boat dock. I would guess one-too-many fun, happy distractions during morning coffee time, prior to departing, was the cause. I called several times, but could not find anyone who gave a hoot about my situation. Good thing that I bought a Goose Feathers cup back in Savanah for memory sake.

Special cups always seem to improve the taste and the morning moment; such as the red cup from Crabby Dick's, given to me by Miss Texas during my stay at the Delaware City Marina. And as I edit this book for the publishers during this COVID Christmas season in 2020, Miss Texas, honored our friendship over the many years, once again, by donating in my name to the Paws of War, whose motto is "Help a Vet**Save a Pet." Animal or human, her Angelic inclination to serve Veterans and their sidekick Pets, who also served, always reveals her natural sweet nature. Or, as I like to think of her, the Mother Theresa for all animals. So hopefully via this book, a worldwide appreciation and thank you revealed for such a thoughtful honor!!!

Anyway, my forgotten cup on Daufuskie Island calls for a someday, curiosity road trip; plus, a ferry boat ride to settle my yearning to retrieve this very special Dad's cup. This island is not available by roads, but Siri and Wikipedia have a very interesting history to tell regarding early humans that called this island home. From this island, Mr. Half-Cup and I proceeded onto Hilton Head and nearby Buford, SC. Like Savannah, both could also become travel habits and never-to-be-forgotten from this coastal area: I discovered she-crab soup, deliberately laced with dry sherry when served. Yum!!!

Another memorable island as well, and only reachable by boat, was Tangier Island in the middle of the Chesapeake Bay. The menu was wonderful crab and more crab. I quickly noticed a cultured dialect to identify with its historical past; plus, the family name Crocket on lots of tombstones in the center-of-town cemetery. That name would naturally catch my attention, since I have spent lots of military time in San Antonio, Texas, and very aware of the history of the Alamo.

From an unusual named island and said to be disappearing; therefore, a visual gage of our slow, but rising sea level, I sailed westerly onto Solomons Island in Maryland and stayed there a month as well. Its connection to the War of 1812 begged the question, why there in delightful Solomons. Up in Lewes, a cannon ball from that war, was left lodged in a building wall near main street. But what caught my eye in nearby Lewes as well, at a viewing area near the entrance to the Bay, a sign that read to my best recall, something like: Thompson, the first family name to settle in Delaware. As I am a third generation Norwegian American and always curious about what occurred at Ellis Island, where my Grandfather Lars Fundlingsland and his bride, Grandma Nora Eik from the Stavanger area of Norway, stepped onto American soil, registered; then walked out the door with the name "Thompson." On my Mother's side, my Grandfather George Leland and his bride, Grandma Martha Ouse came from the Lofoten and Trondheim areas of Norway and kept their spellable names. my question is: Why the name Thompson? Well, lets just go with no one could spell Fundlingsland and chose the Scottish name, Thompson; meaning Son of Thom, Son of Thomas, etc., as per Siri. my Grandfather Dad's name was Thomas; thus, question asked and answered! Frankly, the name Thompson has an amazing track record, with tracks from Delaware, down into the Carolina's, west through Kentucky and Tennessee, onward west through Colorado as noticed on Thompson named ranches west of Denver, then northwest bound and up into British Columbia, judging from the origin and course of the Thompson River. There is even a Thompson, Manitoba and known as the "Hub of the North."

And as I was editing my book, a major news channel paid tribute to a Harriet Thompson, age 92 and still running marathons. Thus, Thompson, a proud "just do it" name and attitude; eventually a coined logo by Nike, surely had its gutsy origins from within the Scottish and Viking heritages. In Prince Rupert, British Columbia, a city with eagles on every street light and otters in the harbor, a monument of Scandinavian Flags stands as a tribute to fellow Vikings who settled the area. Thus, over the years, I proudly flaunted my Viking spirit by sailing from Florida to Maine. And about half way between, I had the luxury to pay my respects for all my Blessings from 45 years in aviation, at Kitty Hawk, North Carolina, where the Wright Brothers did the right thing by me, my life and for the world.

I must admit that I have one Viking flaw, I am not a lutefisk fan; however, my Dad Logan and my Grandparents loved it. Personally, I think it was a crime against a perfect tasting cod fish. Anyway, I failed that third-generation test, but during my sailing era up the east coast, my Viking inclination was to pig out every chance I got on shrimp to the south, on blue crab in the Chesapeake, on lobster to the Canadian border; plus, area clams, mussels, and especially, area specific oysters. Most of these dining delights occurred in and around my Happy Hour addiction and only with a "local" brew. Just add a salad to this diet, and before the summer is over, your underwear will fall off.

But one of the most memorable, "unexpected experiences" popped up on the Intracoastal Waterway between Beaufort and Charleston, South Carolina. Partially mentioned above, fellow Air Force combat vet, Mr. Half-Cup had joined me in Savanah for some "reunion" sailing back to his summer beach home near Cape Fear in North Carolina. He was wounded in Vietnam; yet always exuding his happy-go-lucky demeanor of Baloo, the fatherly bear in the movie, Jungle Boy. As mentioned above, he was my boss during my T-38 era, and he managed like Jesus; thus, to this day all his disciples respectfully call him a forever true friend. Even with his leg wound and with a kind demeanor, he still could beat everyone on the tennis court.

We had refueled at Dataw Island after several days in Hilton Head and in Buford, SC. So, we were thoroughly content and spoiled by then with southern hospitality; thus, we were just planning to anchor out for the next two nights en route to Charleston. Initially, we had been following a faster shrimp boat, but he quickly disappeared into the continually curving intercoastal waterway. Then unexpectedly, we found a totally out of way mom and pop marina, normally used by local shrimpers and their boats. We called on channel 16 and we were directed to tie up behind the very classic shrimp boat that we had been following, to a well weathered, wood-curling dock with a questionable integrity look. Judging from all the loose boards and their rusty nails popping up, probably built before we were both born. The marina itself was classic, southern-aged all the way, and we had to run a hundred-foot-long power cord to find the closest electrical outlet. The marina management was actually within a local grocery store and was also the local daily gossip, community gathering, coffee pot watering hole. The local drawl was a bit strong to grasp what was being said, but the hospitality was clear, comforting and genuine, and in a perfect southern, old-south setting. Bottomline, we bought about three pounds of fresh shrimp right off the boat on our bow. The store apparently owned this shrimp boat and gave us some fresh corn cobs. We put the galley electric double hot plate up on the deck table and within minutes, Mr. Half-Cup and I, enjoyed a lifetime memory, a perfect southern boil, right behind the shrimp boat. How cool is that, sports fans? Definitely another Blessing for both of us, and rest assured that Combat Vets, definitely know where our Blessings come from!!!

A quick preview, but lots of life "stepping stones" to go before I could enjoy those aforementioned, treasured Blessings and none foreseen at this point.

▸▸ The T-38 Flying Sports Car

The Vietnam conflict was still going strong, so Air Force pilot training programs were still going full blast and they trained me as a T-38 Talon Flight Instructor. A supersonic "sports car" with wings, and a fun aircraft that could compete with just about any fighter aircraft in a climb to and above thirty thousand feet. The reason: they, Northrop, used ramjet engines from the Bomarc missile program and it had two.

The Air Force kept me busy, but in December 1970, I simply needed to go home and hug my Dad. He sort-of wanted me to once follow in his footsteps as a farmer and a horse lover. I will always love horses, but hay allergies sort of drove me away from that lifestyle. However, I was told by others that he was rather proud of me as an Air Force pilot and he kept a model of my T-38 on his kitchen shelve, from the days of my thirteen-month flight school. Dad was not big on hugs and verbal "love yuzus'," so I took control of that and went home just to hug him. Truth be known, I was just glad to be alive, considering the past couple of years prior.

my little sister was living with my Dad and I was looking forward to hugging her as well. Now a young lady, I had not seen her, nor my Dad for several years. But low and behold, her best friend, another Eleven, Miss Montana walked in while I was sitting in my Dad's easy chair, reading the book "Love Story." I had recently enjoyed the movie and now with shrinking combat survival memories, I was well primed for new beginnings. Almost prophetic, a true universe, magazine centerfold, eye-popping beauty, who just returned home for the holidays from college in Denver, walked in and changed my life forever. As if she were sent personally from Our Creator Himself. She said that she knew me since she was twelve; well, I knew everything that I needed to know about her in twelve seconds. Plus, my Dad thought of her as family as she grew up next door. One invited trip to their family dinner at a table set for eleven and me, a noticeably Reverent Grace was said as a family, and I felt an oncoming, perfect mix for my life. my life took a pivot from that moment on and that very same book "Love Story," still sits in our china and crystal cabinet, next to the "wedding" cake topper. Yup, another HUGE BLESSING!!!

I never really liked single life even though I had all the girl magnet toys that even included America's car, the Corvette. Since she was my sister's best friend and my Dad adored her, she became a natural, "no brainer" instant improvement to my life. Easiest and smartest decision I would ever make as we were 99.999% compatible; the other 00.001% was because she likes liver and onions. Thus, we were married six weeks after we met, and she "got" the Corvette. This Eleven, came with seven brothers, one younger sister and a resulting bit of rhubarb command in her personality; thus, a perfect Mom for our eventual two Sons and she became a perfect complement to my Air Force career. Soon, we will celebrate 50 years of all Blessings for me and rhubarb pie with a little infusion of natural strawberry sweetener, is still my favorite.

During all that time, another country song always came to mind: "She don't know She's Beautiful" by Sammy Kershaw. Her daily nature and character reflected that in everything she did; especially as a Mom and as a military wife. Her large family upbringing became invaluable, and regardless of dealt situations, she always proceeded with an unflappable mindset while supporting me during my commander-in-charge assignments.

Now obvious that I love country music and every time Tracy Byrd sang his hit song, the "Keeper of the Stars," I felt a family-like energy ensuing to refresh my spiritual development. So instantly enriching to my life as well, my new Mom-in-law, Evelyn, was deeply spiritual. Bless her heart, she visibly lived her Faith and outwardly trusting the Lord. my new Father-in-law, Ernest, had been a WWII POW, so he had my instant, eternal respect as I was a fellow combat veteran. He also had my forever respect for his noteworthy, gentlemen treatment of Mom Evelyn. He would say to her, should the situation dictate, that "after you, I come first!" I wish that I could credit his kind demeanor in a book of famed quotes, as that quote became my mantra of caring for his daughter.

I believe marriage needs daily respect as well as respect to our inner "small" voice to Honor Our Creator; thus, they are mutually linked. Thus, my life pivoted around my Sweetheart of what will be 50 years by the time this book is published. my Sweetheart was a perfect match for my fighter pilot career and my maturity level. She is ten years younger; plus, her outward tiger attitude and spirit fueled my passion to seek whatever zenith that Our Creator "has" in mind for me. Even for my Sweetheart, time moves on, and I will miss her blue-jean cutoffs. I think she finally figured out what was causing babies, and our military budget for cars and housing, suggested two.

Her large family was held together by the Faith of her MOM; Mom Evelyn set the tone for the family spiritual respect of Our Creator and His Son, Jesus. For that alone, I am grateful to the bone, as that tone rubbed off on me!!! I may be the only Son-in-Law that has ever taken his Mother-in-Law to Hawaii on vacation. Yes, just the two of us. She truly deserved my special respect and to taste a bit of paradise here on Our Creator's earth. She got sunburns in places never seen by the Sun before, so mission accomplished. By respecting Mom Evelyn, I was also respecting Our Creator, and to honor Mom Evelyn, I was also Honoring Our Creator. This gradual, renewal respect for Our Creator, brought me back to my childhood need to use Our Creator's eyes to find my lost bag of pennies. By this time in my life, I needed Our Creator's eyes once again; now to refresh, maybe even reboot my life pathway!!! As a timeline, the term "reboot," became the era term to restart computers, so seemed applicable in my life as well.

By this time in my life, I should have been more aware of Our Creator's Blessings, but a little too much into "self" as a result of combat, and reassuring myself daily that I was invincible and the world's greatest fighter pilot. Thus, Our Creator Father had a hard time cracking my typical man shell, but Bless His heart, He was still there, patiently waiting until I started letting Him reenter and run my world. What really opened my eyes as to the patient attentiveness of Our Creator Father, was when my parents got married and enjoyed their honeymoon in a nearby area town hotel. Well, that place was the very same town where my amazing "bride" grew up three blocks away. And for the quick-minded readers, it probably begs the question, how did I know about this town from my past. It so happened that I was also there and born six months later. Thus, every moment of my life that goes by, I am a thousand-percent a voice of and for the "Unborn." As a result, I learned not to generalize in "coincidences," but rather recognize the "Hand" of the "Keeper of the Stars" in our lives; by simply Honoring Our Creator and by giving Him an "open door" to my inner voice.

Nothing like the "Birth of Coolest Son EVER," to put a "proud, grateful Dad" back in touch and stay in touch with one's inner "small" voice; just to say "THANK YOU" a zillion times to Our Father "God"!!! The day prior, around Happy Hour time, Miss Montana, now looking as if she was hiding a large watermelon, did something while in the kitchen and that watermelon broke in the kitchen. Fortunately, it was a Saturday and I was home; so, I got out my Daddy manual and turned to page 110—water broke, head to the hospital. We went to a brand-new hospital and our baby would be baby number two to be born there. We got treated as royalty; however, Mom had to work almost twelve hours before our baby Viking would be born at 4:12AM Sunday morning. She was laying down all night, but for some reason, she was beat. Men can attempt to appreciate, but never fully understand this Creator given, birthing phenomenon. During labor, I mostly remember that anything I said in attempt to be comforting, "was wrong." In those days, it was not an accepted practice that Dads were allowed in the delivery room. So, the nurse brought my noticeably "Stud Viking" to me in a baby warmer. WOW!!! Greatest experience ever!!! The extra care that Mom would need, took an hour plus. Enough time that the image of my muscle-bound, wet, curly-haired Viking, lying there "kickboxing," is still fully entrenched in my memory bank to this day. We sort of expected a boy as he had been kicking for nearly four months. For the record, he still continues to live up to his "Go Gators" attitude on everything that he undertakes. And routinely refreshes his born-with nature through very demanding CrossFit gyms and area marathons.

So, with a super happy, grateful open-door heart and soul, I proceeded through my super pleasing Air Force career. Then flying the snappy T-38 Talon as a flight instructor, and later, the F-4 as a flight instructor as well. All during that time, our "now" family cup "run-eth" over with so many wonderful friends, both here in the US and in Germany. Best of all, all have become one family in Christ Jesus!!! Even till this day, we all still nurture each other with open respect for

Our Creator. "How Great Thou Art" and how great that is, for all of us!!! And probably noticed by now that I generally use three exclamations points each time. That's my way of Honoring the Trinity as well!!! Its my Book, my rules!!! I will also be using occasional run-on sentences when my storyline requires quick sequencing for affect. I prefer to call it, "no time to breathe, excited writing!!!" Again, my Book, my rules!!!

⮞ **F-4 to Thailand**

During this period, follow-on Air Force assignments led to traveling opportunities around Thailand, and later, Europe. Thailand was essentially my second combat tour to the Vietnam theatre, this time in the F-4 Phantom. The F-4 was initially designed as a Navy fleet interceptor; thus, the name Phantom—as in coming out of nowhere and undetected. It was also rigorously built to withstand carrier landings; thus, it became a workhorse airplane for the Navy, the Marines and big time for the Air Force as well. It was not a pretty airplane, but it had the kick-ass look of a Rhino. We all pretty much thought of it as "big bad ugly" and those two J-79's made lots of respectful noise.

As a result of my flying experiences, I was chosen as a Functional Flight Check Pilot for aircraft coming out of heavy maintenance, which meant that I often got to fly a totally clean F-4. I had that position at both my Thailand base and later, my Florida base. During my time as a F-4 Instructor in Florida, I and my WSO would do all our flight checks out over the Gulf. There we had access to all altitudes and all speeds; so, while checking a clean, relatively new F-4E model to see if it would measure up to its design specs, an opportunity entered my mind.

So, once we reached near Mach 2 within the engine envelope, I pulled her straight up and watched the vertical velocity instrument peg at over 6000 feet per minute. She approached zero airspeed somewhere close to 65,000 feet. We were definitely approaching Our Creator's balcony of deeper blue skies. But we were not properly appareled for this altitude, so I was too busy watching and keeping the engines running. We could lose one, but not both. It was best just to let her fall where she may and not interfere with the air flow through her engines until her nose pointed downhill. By the way, I treated all airplanes as girls; probably enough said on that subject.

My everyday F-4 flying in Northern Thailand was business as usual in support of the Vietnam conflict and my free time turned out to be a wonderful time to discover the inner souls of the Thailand people. The entire time I was in Thailand, I felt totally safe everywhere I went; normally traveling via full trains. Such trips included the northwest areas near Burma, where I searched for Burmese jade for my Sweetheart; now mostly decorating our safety deposit box. Little did I know that I would be Blessed with a spectacular Granddaughter 40 years later. She will make this jade jewelry look spectacular as well. The central areas and down to Bangkok were essentially rural as well; sort of felt like the rural areas of my youth. I will never forget the elephant races. Apparently, a weekend enjoyment like USA drag or horse racing.

While hanging out with the Thai people, I was reminded of similar events and lifestyles back in North Dakota. As a kid around age ten or eleven, and at the county fair horse races, riding bareback, I fell off my horse at the finish line no less. I won the race, or at least my horse won, and did not get a bruise, nor a bump from all horses to my rear. Never was sure why I fell off, but it got crowded near the finish line and recall lots of quirt use on both sides. I would never use, nor needed to use a quirt or long bridal straps on any of my childhood horses, as they were my friends as well. Plus, my Dad would have used it on me. However, I cannot imagine falling off an elephant without a post life complication, but it was the big cultural game in town there in Thailand.

Even during my first tour, I felt safe all over the Philippines, and in Taiwan and Hong Kong as well. The only place I did not feel safe was during my jungle survival training in the Philippines, with all those green vipers and spitting cobras. Our combat training mission was to avoid getting caught by the local tribesmen, while spending one night among the jungle rats and snakes. Still have thoughts about that night, and in my mind, more dangerous than combat or going to the moon. But by using Native American Indian lore and hiding my trail, I never got caught. During my youth, my heroes and subsequent childhood desired studies were all about Native Americans like War Chief Crazy Horse, and famous mountain men like Jim Bridger and Jeremiah Johnson. And it paid off during my time in the jungle.

Nevertheless, my walkaway Far-East travel impressions noted two of the oldest religions at play. Since the Vietnam conflict was dialing down, it became a wonderful time to enjoy the local culture as well as hunt for unique jewelry for my Sweetheart. Well deserved, since she had made my life absolutely "perfect" with the birth of our first of two sons. How Blessed can one man be, has been my everlasting assessment and with forever gratefulness to Our Creator.

While in the Thailand region, I witnessed firsthand the religions of the area at the people level. Religions are man-made as a result of innumerable factors over decades of communal issues and daily life needs. Nothing like a train ride from northern Thailand to Bangkok to frame my thoughts of the everyday life and the demeanor of the people; they were wonderfully, innately kind to me and offered to feed me local treats. For the benefit of my potential readers, beyond firsthand "boots" on the ground knowledge while on location, the majority of my research into specific religions started with Siri and then into Wikipedia. What evolved in my heart and soul, is that Our Creator "Daddy" has a lot of very nice kids, whom all bleed red and have "interchangeable parts." The Far East religions became tied to visible idols over time to show outward, mutual respect to their inner spiritual voices and to foster a communal nirvana. I did not sense any heathenism nor paganism, but a cultured respect, which also evolved over time for our Native Americans as well. Their outward mutual respect for the white buffalo, and/or respect for "thee" earth mother, was surely in response to their inner spiritual voice. Siri said that "all Native Americans see the entire universe as being alive," and I as well, sensed the same among Native Americans. Bottom line, they always had my deepest respect.

Bottom line, Our Creator never created religions, only mankind created what became defined as religions and none should be judged as heathen or pagan. Unless, they did, or do human sacrifices; which then would be contrary and insulting to Our Creator as creator's create, not destroy. What is respect to Our Common "Daddy" by one person or group, often becomes defined and/or judged as a religion by another. Typically expected from

hypocrites, or the politically adrift, and probably the most annoying "sinners" of all in the eyes Our Creator. Once the self-righteous criticize, attempt to influence, or judge others, and then stray from their "inner 'small' voices," a "cult" is then birthed. They then run the risk of losing their credibility to serve Our Creator, the Father of "All." We, or they all pay respects in our, or their own way, to our very same "Daddy" of all communal groups and worldwide areas for a multitude of reasons. But "we" all have common grounds and values, as revealed in Neanderthal burial sites. And to be clear, I would rather use the word "rejectors," vice "sinners" and will clarify during my continued storyline.

▸▸ F-4 Flight Instructor

Shortly after flying what may have been the last F-4 mission over Saigon itself and our Embassy evacuation on April 30, 1975, I was reassigned to Florida to become an F-4 Flight Instructor. Although this farm boy loved the western mountains, and their darling trout streams and their incredible ski slopes, this roughened westerner found a unique paradise in Florida. Even as I write this book, forty-five years later, and now that I have seen the world, I still feel and think that I truly did find an earth paradise.

Here we built a house from scratch on a canal, and shortly after moving in, my Sweetheart Blessed me with Son number two. Hurrah!!! Hurrah!!! Now I had a Son for each arm. This one rarely kicked in the hangar, so sort of expected a girl. Nevertheless, this cuter-than-words can express, Baby Viking, flew into our lives during Happy Hour prices. This time, Dad was allowed to be a part of the arrival party, and I don't recall that Mom even broke a sweat. This birthing hospital was so cool; even a gourmet dinner was included with the routine stay. And a little over thirty years later, more Blessings, our three Grandchildren would be born in this very same hospital, complements of Son number one and Miss Florida. A catchy fact; our Son number one was born in Tempe, AZ; while our Son number two was born in Tampa, FL. But shortly after Son number two was born and still in diapers, Dad got orders to Europe.

⏭ **Europe**

So, with a three-year old and a baby, we departed for Europe, the same day that Elvis Presley passed, a never to be a forgotten timeline. Even with living in Florida and a home in a paradise setting, who would turn down a trip to Europe. It would mean a future trip to Norway to visit our heritage for starters, but it would also become a part of our life forever with a new evolving family of German friends. Boy, did my Sweetheart have her Mom-hands full! Actually, she handled it like the champ that she has always been; plus, completing all her college entry requirements from the University of Maryland extensions in Europe. Our two Sons stole the hearts of all our European friends, and became able to converse in German, became ready-to-rock snow skiers and became world-aware travelers. What totally pleased me were two trips to Norway. The first was a camping trip through Germany, Denmark, Sweden and throughout the southern half of Norway. my Sweetheart found her relatives around the Oslo area and I found my relatives around the Stavanger area. With a car trunk full of camping gear, a tent and tons of diapers, we intermingled with so many fun European travelers in their camping grounds. They were mostly families, all young and trying to save money like us; all with common values and neighborly attitudes. They were noticeably envious of our large trunk on our 1973 Monte Carlo.

For my second trip, my Dad and Mom Evelyn came over to Germany in the weather-pleasant month of July. Then after a few days of time change acclimation and lots of love-energy absorbing hugs from their Grandsons, we departed by train from northern Bavaria to northern Norway, with Mom Evelyn staying with relatives around the Oslo area. my Dad and I continued north of the Arctic Circle to the coastal town of Bodo, with a slash through the trailing "o." We were amazed to see farming above the Arctic Circle and more amazed to enjoy eating a snack on a dock facing the North Sea at 2 AM, under rather bright sunny skies. my Dad Logan, was a second generation Norwegian, so it was such a pleasure for me to honor my Dad with a trip to where his Mom Nora and his Dad Lars were born and raised in Norway. It was his eventual reward for training me to work hard and never quit until I achieved my quest. And that was my message to an overflowing crowd at his interment ceremony, in a church roughly six blocks from the hotel where my parents enjoyed their honeymoon. Yup, I attended both!!!

Serving in Bavaria did eventually near the three-year point, and as expected, a new assignment would return me to the F-4 cockpit as a Wild Weasel pilot. So, Florida and our rented-out-house would need to wait, while my Air Force Era continued onto California. More Blessings followed for everyone during our five-year assignment in southern California. The flying was beyond fantastic, my Sweetheart got her Nursing degree, Son number one became a computer wizard with his new Texas Instruments version, and Son number two became a desert lizard expert. Son number two had figured out the biology facts of life rather quickly from his passion for animals, etc. Thus, one of his life curiosity questions still sticks in my mind, when he asked while we were driving our new car, an 8-6-4 engine Biarritz. He was around five and he was still able to stand behind me with his arms hugging me at the time, and asked, "Dad, I know how to get a wife and how to get kids, but how do you get a car?"

Our high desert home had a large rear picture window of the picturesque San Bernardino Mountains. This daily observable Blessing afforded our family with the close-by opportunities to continue improving our family skiing, which had begun in Europe. For me, occasionally running into legends Roy Rogers and Dale Evans, who lived nearby in their Apple Valley home, will also stick in my fond memories, along with all the T-ball games that filled my "Dad" heart with feelings of being Blessed.

Eventually, we would return to our Florida home on a waterfront canal, just the exact opposite of our California home. So glad that we did not sell our Florida home prior to our European assignment. Blessed because my two Super Sons grew up in this house and now my Double Super Grandchildren also enjoy this unique house location. We paid thirty-eight thousand for it new. So glad that I recognized its paradise potential then, as its current waterfront value is now over ten times and probably would not be available. As it turned out, it was money well spent for my family future. As I compose this book about Blessings, the current value house payment would surely have put a huge dent in our retirement budget, so I see that as a Blessing as well!!!

When we retired from the Air Force, we remodeled it with flavors of Europe and Santa Fe, NM, on the inside, as we have our Florida paradise on the outside. Thus, I so enjoy the mesmerizing water flow, with occasional moments of "stars dancing on the water," in the canal thirty feet away; thus, aiding the fostering of my thoughts for this book to Honor Our Creator. Siri told me that I am 2026 miles from where I lost my bag of pennies, but indubitably provided me a perfect setting to sense and to think in "Blessings" to "birth" this book. I can expect to see daily dolphins and manatees swim by; plus, an occasional otter that stirs my recall of all the otters playing along the Pacific shores. If you saw the movie, Golden Pond, you would have enjoyed it. I sure did and now enjoy our family-owned Golden Canal. Ponds are enclosed, but canals usually lead somewhere and out our back door, from our boat slip, to anywhere in the world of open waters, is now available. Much like the freedom of soaring a fighter aircraft skyward, through the shades of blue, I found a freedom to sail out the canal to Norway, should I wish—and now our sailboat, the Nurse T & Skipper Me is in Bar Harbor, Maine. Yes, this is paradise on earth to me and close enough for this farm boy. Yes, it tells me that Our Creator Father was definitely listening back when I was looking for my lost bag of pennies!!!

I have grown to love thinking about Our Creator and His Universe, His planet earth and our Florida home in terms of Blessings. But back to August 1977, and once again, all these "now" Blessings came with "stepping stones." Florida would need to wait, since the Berlin wall was still up and with tense situations still going on, my mind was still on my duty to my country. I was reassigned to Europe as an Air Force liaison with our US Army Command, charged with guarding the US segment of the fenced wall between the two Germanys. What a wonderful opportunity to enjoy years of history and struggles. I was the commander of a small unit to coordinate Air Force support, and my second in command, or sergeant-in-charge, was a 1956 immigrant from Hungary, via Austria, who spoke all the area languages. It's a pleasure to include scribed tributes for all our family Blessings that we so appreciated while in Europe. For starters, what a gift our European-born staff member, Tony, and his family were throughout our European tour of duty to my family there in northern Bavaria. Tony made my daily responsibilities a cakewalk.

Also, daily, wonderfully uplifting church bells in our surrounding area would remind me of their scripted Crosses with INRI imprinted and of course, Our Savior Jesus!!! Our classic Bavarian abode was less than twenty miles from where Martin Luther did his thing inside a cool castle and a stone's throw from the fenced border. Thus, I found it easy "not" to forget Our Creator with so much outward respect shown over the decades through the area churches. How important to credit Our Creator Father for all our family Blessings: We got to see Norway, my heritage homeland twice; and so very important to me, shared with my Dad and Mom Evelyn. And still going strong, our loved, memorable and still appreciated to this day, are all our Bavarian acquaintances, now our extended family. They are to this day, now over 40 years later, still totally, genuine family friends!!! The eventual worldwide internet and now simple texting with pictures, has helped us stay close in thought and with an internalized family spirit.

The age tested, enormous respect for the Deity of Our Creator was enjoyably apparent in all the church architecture and carried into the conduct of the church as well. Our travels all over Europe and through the Vatican, to include the Notre Dame, seemed to have been an era of seemingly competitive church building and their period of construction was often years, or longer than the lives of their designers and builders. Such outward dedication to Our Deity, Our Creator, was definitely an enjoyable and respectful experience.

As I was Air Force and not generally involved in daily Army affairs, I decided to use my free time to acquire a law degree affiliated with the California Bar and Illinois Bar. my time thinking about Our Creator was pretty much relegated to enjoying and respecting his presence in all the beautiful cathedrals during our tour in Europe. I needed to begin prepping for my departure from the Air Force, so becoming a corporate pilot/corporate attorney seemed to be a plausible endeavor. I had enough free time to get straight "A's" while in Europe, but upon my return to my new US assignment, I took the bar exam cold and missed the passing grade by a few.

Nevertheless, what a unique time for me and my family, in Europe amidst so much history of influencing religions; plus, studying the beginnings of our common law, or king "made" law. and of course, all the skiing in the nearby Alps, that included totally, forever memorable nights sleeping over the cows in Austria. The heat emitted from the cows below, kept the upper loft warm as warm air rises; how clever and how quaint. I had milked my first cow when I was around eight back on our family North Dakota farm, so I was right at home and even the familiar fragrances of my past, were an enjoyable part of the ambiance. And happily repeating, since so very important to me, two trips to Norway, for me to take my family one year by car, a 1973 Monte Carlo. Then the next year, my Dad and my Mom Evelyn—totally unforgettable—by train like three college kids with back packs, so cool—Thank You, Sir Viking Odin, or Our Creator, Amen!!!

▸▸ F-4 Wild Weasel Time

my European job was nonflying except for enjoying occasional rides with the Army and their Apache choppers, and a ride with the German Air Force in their F-104's. WOW, a rocket that flew like a dream!

Then onto my next flying assignment in southern California, near Apple Valley, the home of Roy Rogers and Dale Evans from my comic book days and black and white tv era. They were so nice and so into supporting the local community. Prementioned prior, but important to note that this area was so compatible for my family as I watched my precious Sons benefit from local sports programs and from great teachers that surely set the stage for Son number one to excel later in "all" his noteworthy, successful endeavors. Thank You, Carol! Plus, my Sweetheart was able to continue and tidy up her desires to become a Nurse, and graduated from a nearby College of Nursing. Prementioned as well, that this assignment came with those unforgettable, snowcapped, mountains and the view out our then backside living room windows; much like our current view out our now waterside windows. Both situations are still embraced with the same level of appreciation and equal Blessings, then and now!!!

my new squadron of high time F-4 drivers were in the process of a Wild Weasel mission transition from the famed F-105 Thud into the updated F-4G, my Rhino. Same mission, but with new equipment for new threats and a new training area for me, called

Red Flag, or after my Air Force retirement, the real-world Desert Storm. Prior to Desert Storm and while I was still in the Air Force, I had the unforgettable pleasure of working for a noticeably more-cultured, "well honed" General. First and foremost, he was an exemplary Officer and a highly experienced Fighter Pilot. But for me, it was his speaking eloquence and his clear penning of his leadership expectations of me and his command. This subtle beneficial experience was both timely and valuable as I now owned a law degree; that I planned to use upon my retirement. Thus, he was incidentally mentoring my communication skills, he introduced me to lots of dollar words and two-dollar phrases, and better yet, he gave me command of an Air Force training unit called Air Warrior. It was a perfect job match for me as I had flown 254 combat support sorties for both the Army and Marines in Vietnam; plus, recently returned from Germany where I enjoyed a liaison role with the "peacetime" Army unit responsible for the US segment of the Berlin Wall. The Air Warrior mission was to provide Air Force assets and to train both Air Force and Army aviators for seamless deployment of air power assets. And to reboot post-Vietnam thinking and its jungle-like environment, to desert thinking and in an all-desert environment. Guess what, we were so ready for Operation Desert Storm! Our use of air power was so effective that according to Siri, our ground war only lasted around 100 hours.

During Desert Storm, I was actually in the Seven-4-Seven, or Boeing 747, and flying military warriors in and out of the middle east support bases. As a supporting flight crew, I was privy to the Operation Desert Shield area air control plan around the "hot" area and immediately recognized the copycat plan from my Air Warrior command. For the curious, check out You Tube and my previous 56lst Tactical Fighter Squadron, who were deployed to the Gulf War, to do what Wild Weasels' do with their F-4G's. The mission motto remained "First In, Last Out!' and tasked to blind the enemy and keep him blinded.

So above, I just previewed the very essence of my next aviation assignment and mission after returning home from my European assignment, another Blessing, this time a big WOW! I would be doing what I stated above, or prepping for what Wild Weasels' do. It was all Top Gun flying! Wild and exciting, intensive low-level flying with the throttles in the far-left corner; thus, smokin' at corner velocity to 600 knots, and where else, at tree top level. Sure scared up lots of wild horses in our training areas, and my awareness altimeter was if I could make out actual horse ears or tree leaves, I was too low. Then with crisp teamwork quarterbacking from Randy, my super rear seat weapons systems officer, we pop up, roll upside down, nose and cursor on target and say hello to the enemy! Next, continue to stay alert for air-to-air entanglements going in and out of the target arena. Always loved the movie "Top Gun" and this Wild Weasel flying was that and more! Now that was "cool," full throttle, full use of the side view egg-look, energy-egg flying. From full burner airspeeds at tree tops to zero airspeed at the top of the egg, there I was for the moment, lame duck vulnerable to any aggressor air players, but with a birds-eye view and still in the game.

We continually prepped, knowing that we would be "First In," and as such, we would always be included in any practice wartime scrimmage. Whether it be in our USA training areas or somewhere in the world. We would deploy where needed, whether it was practice or real. my Squadron, the 561st did just that, so I and my highly specialized WSO, or Weapons Systems Officer, flew nonstop from California to Germany. We took our entire squadron herd of F-4G Weasels and followed several airborne fuel tankers. I have since forgotten the flight time, but the thirteen airborne hookups for gas are still fresh in my memory bank. Over my fighter pilot career, I am quite certain that I "hooked up for gas," over three hundred times; thus, this capability gives our USA Air Force an immeasurable advantage, whether it be in the worldwide deployment phase, or in the battle arena, as in Desert Storm in 1991.

Thank You, Air Force, you were wonderful to me, you Blessed me beyond my wildest dreams or imagination. I would depart with tons of Fighter/T-38 trainer flying time. And I would depart with three college degrees as well: a bachelor's degree in accounting, a master's degree in management and a law degree. I should be ready to tackle the other world of "whatever." I had acquired my Airline Transport Rating, or ATP after I returned from Europe, and I took my FAA rating ride in Johnny Carson's Lear 24. A real honor for me at the time, as he was a famed nighttime TV host. At that moment in time, my only plan was to retake the bar exam; and this time, get some prep help to pass. But with Faith and my airline class date, Scene II slipped into Scene III in one weekend. With close family-like friends, and I mean close, so close that we had become pajama-level friends during our mutual tours in Europe. Our close family-like friendship evolved as result of military stairwell housing, to include same aged children and similar military agendas as well. I was Air Force, and my stairwell counterpart was Army. His mission agenda was all about air defense, as in from the ground up, and boy, did that mission evolve into the highest level of importance till this very day. Thus, my close stairwell friend, Mr. Army, went on to be essentially the father of the Israel Iron Dome as a result of his trusted leadership during Desert Storm. So, with two-pound T-Bones, we celebrated my 24 wonderful years with the Air Force on a Friday night and then I started my Airline Career on Monday morning.

SCENE

III

my Airline Era

During my airline job interview, which I attended a month before I actually retired, I handed my Air Force flight records to the interviewer. And after about five minutes of looking through my extensive stick-time flying file, he observed not one hour of autopilot time; then asked only one question: "when can you start?" So, I said in a month and he gave me a class date.

The aviation atmosphere went from serious-serious to serious-fun in a flash. Back then, newbies generally started as Flight Engineers, or no-stick time pilots. I felt like a fraternity pledge once again, but the atmosphere was warmed by teamwork decorum and respected crew relevance. I had to retrain my cockpit mindset from single-seat self to crew. I became a crew "Mr. checklist" reader, a common beginning among new guy airline aviators, regardless of prior experience, type aircraft or crew mission.

The airlines typically use seniority bidding for determining where all pilots will be used to crew all aircraft fairly and the pay associated with the aircraft one receives from the bid. Well, about two months after I began my airline flying, I once again was Blessed to receive a DC-10 copilot slot in Honolulu, Hawaii. Wow! I just went from a F-4 cockpit height to a DC-10 co-pilot cockpit height; what a Cadillac airplane! Electric seats! Then after a couple of later aircraft bids, to a B-747 co-pilot cockpit height of twenty-nine feet above the tarmac. I barely flared the F-4 on landing, now think about the B-747 landing flare with all those wheels. The B-747 was such an impressive airplane and I so enjoyed eight wonderful years of covering the globe. And with memories such as, Phillip Island, still south of Melbourne, Australia, where I was underdressed for the occasion. All the penguins wore their black formal tuxes, paid us never-no-mind and wondered all around us, while returning from their daily swim and dine, to their nests with a view. The B-747 is one the largest aircraft ever and I could stand up inside its engine. Yet, still the best advice to land the B-747, fly it like a Piper Cub, but start the flare planning at around a hundred feet. Also consider yourself a member of the eighteen-wheeler truck driver's club, sixteen wheels on the main landing gear and two on the nose gear.

‣ **The 747**

Flying International Co-Pilot on a B-747, or DC-10; then later as Captain on the B767, one spends considerable time at around 35,000 feet. Actually, it's a perfect quality time to Honor Our Creator and His Majesty!!! You get to enjoy observing Haley's Comet near the Southern Cross back in 1986, while en route to Australia or New Zealand; or, the dancing northern lights while en route to Europe. So not to waste such precious time, I enrolled in a Bible course with Liberty University. The majority of the course study was by listening to tapes, so no conflict with my cockpit scan awareness. For those readers wondering why I was studying by listening, rather than just watching the flights instruments, it is well known that one may miss a pending issue when staring. But any change, especially, a flashing warning light or any light change will be noticed quicker if not staring at an instrument panel during the wee hours.

Prior to my airline career, I nibbled at the Bible from time-to-time with typical verse awareness, but learned very little about Our Creator's Deity and Personality Nature as Our Father figure. After considerable amount of global travel awareness of all the cultures and their area religions, I challenged myself to honor my Uncle Elwood and Mom Evelyn, my Sweetheart and my precious Sons by Honoring Our Creator. Thus, I read the Good News version of His "Word" cover-to-cover twice and twice more except for speed-reading all the begats, Chronicles, Judges and Kings. Reading Our Creator's Word cover to cover was first baited by a Readers Digest version that was composed as a novel. That "novel" idea was so powerful and priceless in trail blazing a clear, contiguous understanding of Our Creator's Thesis. After reading the Readers Digest version, I became totally hooked on reading Our Creator's Word cover to cover, but now with a pre-awareness of Our Creator's lighted pathway for my life hereafter. After dining on sixty-six Bible books several times, one can walk away with a feel for Our Creator's timing and issues, both before and during, in composing His Word. His Authorship theme as Our Creator, and His Thesis assertions, from which, His intentions began to shine through loud and clear; like any author composition outline. Our Creator Father's timing and His means to compose also became understandable and clear. Actual Pastors, Priests and probably the Rabbis, would probably poo-poo my reading of the Readers Digest novel version of Our Creator's Word, but they surely went to their seminary and they were surely brain cultured like a Marine. However, Jesus, did not go to seminary, but did facilitate and render His Gospel CliffsNotes to Our Creator's Word in such verses as John 3;16 and John 19;30. For me, these verses are two super clear, total enchiladas, but for the confused, hang your hat on Matthew 17;20 until you wise up.

Quick Siri research revealed that signs of respectful awareness of Our Creator was discovered among Neanderthals burial sites, but Our Creator waited until the situation of the Egyptian nation and their enslavement of the Jewish nation to reveal Himself outwardly. The Egyptian culture and respect to their inner perceived deity was manifested in idols. The enslaved Jews, in my Opinion, became the chosen people of Our Creator as they were, by their predicament, now situation needy, and now inner "small" voice reachable; thus, Spiritually accessible as well. Since Our Creator is Our Spiritual Father,

He finally had a compatible, workable spiritual relationship with His human creation. Other human settlements around Our Creator's planet were probably dealing with daily and visual survival issues; yet, more content, at least content with tangible idols, and less attentive to Our Creator's outreach. However, the Jewish nation was residing in an arid topography, enslaved and struggling as in "needy." And timing wise, the Egyptians had advanced a "means" for Our Creator to compose His "Word." Our Creator now had the use of papyrus and later paper, for lay scribes to record Our Creator's Revelations by honoring their inner "small" voices and then scribed onto storable scrolls for eventual illumination.

I got a big fat "F" on my first college composition, but Our Creator got an 'A+' on His first composition via His Spiritually influenced dictation to numerous faithful and inspired scribes; all from different walks of life and over several decades and years. From their scrolls found in several locations around Our Creator's Holy Land, summarily became Our Creator's everlasting "Word." Eventually, all their decades of efforts would become collected, seemingly chronicled except for the Book of Job, which is thought to be the oldest book. And then canonized into "66" Books and finally, Our Creator's Outreach Bible. Siri stated that the word "Bible" is Greek for "papyrus plant;" thus, subtly authenticating Our Creator's authorship time line. Not surprising, all Our Creator's individual books dove tailed perfectly after collected and canonized. The Dean of my Liberty University Bible School and his Bible course, Dr. H.L. Wilmington, astutely assessed that "the Bible is a book that man would not write if he could, and could not write if he would."

No need to elaborate that summation as I could not if I would. Suffice to say that Our Creator's "Word" has stood the test of time from probably thousands of critiquing individuals with thousands of different motives. The only thing about the Bible that I never understood, why do the Gideons hand out Bibles written in the Queen's English to the homeless and wayward; yes, I did work with the Gideons. A college graduate that majored in English would have a difficult time grasping Our Creator's message written as such. As an airline pilot, I spent lots of time in hotels, so I usually checked the bedside table drawer just to sense the local respect paid to Our Creator. It's takes a degree from Oxford to understand that style of writing and after one or two verses, the free Bible is most likely never read, set aside or thrown away if a street person.

Thus, well intentioned efforts may never get to reveal that Our Common Daddy, only wants to reveal his Goodness, His Grace and His Love as in the Book of Job; plus, where my book is heading to reveal my personal desire to Honor Our Creator, as did Job. Job paid tribute to His Redeemer, Job 19:25, and I wish to complement his tribute by Honoring my Creator Daddy.

Job's Faith was demonstrably out the roof, but as stated in the Gospels, that "belief" in the size of a mustard seed will guarantee eternal life with Our Creator Father by simply asking prayerfully, which then activates Our Creator Father's binary Positive Spiritual Nature. Plus, no perfection or works required!!! Religions love to throw in qualifiers, but Sir Jesus simply said "Love Thy Father and Love Thy Neighbor!!!" Then, Sir Jesus further "Cliffs noted" His Gospels with John 3:16, and then by design credence, guaranteed His Gospels at the Cross, with John 19:30. Sir Jesus understood His Father, kept His Gospels messages clearly binary, and that Our Creator responds to binary Faith, Hope, Trust, and above all, Love. And of course, always a binary open door as well to total forgiveness!!!

I love Bibles that can be read like a novel, but Our Creator's authored Book was Spiritually dictated to numerous scribes over several hundred years and from a myriad of backgrounds. Then considering the recording means and the storage preservation means, I think we are fortunate to have what we have. Especially, so amazingly accurate, totally coherent; and when added up, a hundred percent reliable manuscript from Our Creator. Great Job, Father!!!

As I compose this book, and my blog-a-book, or e-book, through my website endeavor, the area north and northeast of the Armageddon area; aforementioned in the last book of Our Creator's "Word," or Revelations, is struggling with nearby religion impacted conflicts. These conflicts have both political and territorial aspirations within an ancient religion that could easily boil or spill over into Father's foreseen vulnerable, apocalyptic theatre near Megiddo, in Israel. It's simply amazing that Our Creator's "Word," written over centuries ago, is still batting a hundred percent accuracy. That in itself suggests Our Creator's involvement. For the curious, the Donkey has something to say about that—more to follow.

During my Bible study at 35,000 feet, and lots of starring into clear space, you find a new clarifying logic developing within your soul. Just as Gene Cernan, the last astronaut to have walked on the moon, reportingly said, which I may have somewhat paraphrased, that "there are no atheists in outer space." Even Einstein concluded that the complexity of our incredible universe had its beginnings bestowed by a super incredible Creator of and why E=mc2 functions throughout our Universe. But one thing became crystal clear to me as I studied, mentally uninterrupted, among the incredible view of the stars; that they maybe shining on "their" planets as well, and "that" visible clarity would be: Our Creator did not create religions; nor, that "Honoring Our Creator" is a religion. But rather by honoring our inner "still or small" voice, as created within all humanoids, "is" our spiritual connection to Our Creator Daddy, or to "His Image." And most likely via a Spiritual "Energy" Connection that actually created all that "is" within His Universe; either visible or invisible, either tangible or intangible during His "In the Beginning."

Only mankind created religions for a multitude of what probably started as good reasons, and I readily noticed during my world travels among the older religions, that they and their followers have more in common than what separates them. What separates religions and, in many cases, just like their governments, is simply mankind politics. Mankind political differences over time, can burden common causes, can splinter and even separate the religions from within and cause get-a-long issues; such as with current Islam and its paradox situation: the "peace be upon you" religion; yet the conflicted Shiites and the Sunnis. The recent ISIS Caliphate situation only-goes-to-prove that mankind can screw up anything Our Positive Creator desires for His Kids, with their negative influencing ego causes and politics. Our Creator gave each of His Kids an inner "small" voice and their chosen religions may offer great social gatherings for sharing, but equally important to respect your personal inner "small" voice as Our Common Daddy's way keeping all of us on the straight and narrow!!! His Word says Live Positive and Believe even if minimally, as in the Size of a "mustard seed," and Trust. Plus, my word says: follow the Donkey to total Belief and visual Blessed Assurance!!!

Cruising in the lower altitudes of the stratosphere and the upper troposphere, colder, thinner air lessens drag and optimizes fuel endurance, and when trimmed out at .85-87 Mach, became a perfect classroom to study Our Creator's Word. The majority of my international flights were at night, so that we would arrive early morning for the customer's benefit. Generally, around thirty-five thousand feet, the resulting night-time views were incredible. And like my "in the beginning" that I laid out back in Scene I and now here in Scene III, His Word came to life and stirred new mind-wondering. Our Creator's Universe and Our surrounding Galaxy is so cool; that it's near impossible not to mind-wonder while looking out at Our Creator's stage. For me, additional thoughts and words began to enter the explanation of OUR CREATOR'S "IN THE BEGINNING!"

Recorded works and words of Aristotle and, more recent of course, words by Einstein began to become vividly at play. However, these two names are only two among several mentioned in a Wikipedia "lite" research. As my aviation career involved an "energy" awareness; especially, during my fighter pilot era and the use of the "energy egg" during air-to-air encounters. And then again, when taking off in an eight to nine-hundred-thousand-pound B-747 and then finding the commonly termed "in step" airspeed for the best fuel flow and corresponding range. Energy conscious at all times, I generally flew faster than most in order to keep the wing leading edge looking downhill and less drag. Result: as the fuel weight lightened, throttling back saved fuel and rewarded customers with earlier arrivals.

⇥ Energy Perceptions

Flying at night, one can generally become mesmerized by mind-starring at stars and their associated constellations. Flying during daylight, one can mind-stare into infinite space. In either situation, one can mind-associate the word "energy" and all its many adaptations, interpretations, manifestations and relationships everywhere you look. It began to become an innate, or an instinctive explanation of Our Creator. Bottomline, I would not be flying without energy and moreover, I and our mother earth would not be here without "energy." The word "energy" had not evolved during the composing and canonizing of Our Creator's Word; even though Aristotle began its use around 350BC.

I have never heard any religious leader or scientist use the word creator and the word energy in the same sentence. Why and/or why not? When I connect the dots, it seems inherently obvious; so, the rest of my book—"will" head in that direction. For the religious types, how could our Universe and all within be created without an "energy elixir". Scientists almost say it, but the word religion seems to get in their way, as if there is no connection. Better yet, just think that Our Creator, so totally capable of multitasking, created all energy forms through "His Spiritual Energy Form Entity," as "it takes one to know one." An idiom that I borrowed to clarify simple logic. Since they cannot rule out Our Creator, they seem to think that if they take the antithesis approach, they may have greater credibility. And that's bull, since the Laws of Energy, nothing gained, nothing lost within His Universe, clearly connects Our Creator to the equation and never forget, His Energy is Transmutable. A big word for a capability, or an ability to change in form, nature, substance to another and yet, never lost.

Since Our Creator did not create religions, I sense just the opposite and propose that they are just stubbornly human and may actually support each other, but too proud to hold hands. Our Creator's "IN THE BEGINNING" enthralls or captures our attention as to "whom" are we trying to identify, or "who" is this Entity that started all that "is," both visible and invisible, and all that "is" both tangible and intangible. I repeat often for emphasis that Our Creator's Word tells us that we are created "in His image," and that He can, or will tickle our minds via our inner "small" voice. We were created with the power of choice; thus, we can honor that "tickle" nudge or reject. That certainly sounds like a Spiritual Entity to me, and since He lives in my Heart and Soul, if I should wish to hug him, I guess I just externally hug myself. Not to be coy, but rather the opposite, as Our Creator is as he said, I AM, IAM!!! Most of Our Creator's Word uses the term "God." but since this book is about my awareness of several religions, I chose to use the term Creator. There is only one Creator and guess what, we all have the very same Creator "Daddy." We all bleed red and we all have interchangeable body parts. and, there are innumerable uses of the term "god," but only one common understanding or use of the word, Creator.

The one word that I wish to affiliate or connect to Our Creator in this book, is the word that I have eluded to above and that is the word "Energy." Our Creator Father is commonly agreed to be a "SPIRIT" Entity and His Son, JESUS, confirmed that in His Gospels. From my occasional advantage point at thirty-five thousand feet, I perceive Our Creator to be a powerful "Spiritual Energy" Entity. That connection clarifies everything I see and everything that I read, regardless of source, Amen!!!

The question is: Have I missed something from my readings or understanding of this seemingly obvious personal conclusion. That just seems too obvious to have "not" been connected all these years by both religious leaders and scientists. Probably just domain selfishness?? Nonetheless, it seems blatantly obvious and explains all that "is" in my purview, in 37 seconds. All the amazing Energy Laws, Nature Laws and their creation theories become relative and understandable throughout our Universe and right down to our own personal body. When I study planet and star compositions, I find that our mother earth and our personal bodies have numerous common elements and most notably, our water relationships. And I can read about most of them on the back of a multivitamin bottle, so when our Creator's Word says that He used the "soil of the earth to form man;"

then "breathed into our nostrils," He was not kidding, or oversimplifying!!! And He simply used or added his common elements called oxygen and nitrogen to give us functional animated abilities. Thus, man is composed of all the elements commonly found on, or in our mother earth, and also profoundly interesting, nearly in the same water percentages as our mother earth. Water is a vital and natural planet energy conduit for Our Creator to connect with our neural circuitry; then trigger or respond via Spiritual Energy, in my Opinion, to our inner "small" voice—more on that to follow.

Equally profound is Our Creator's means to continue growing His creations through our females, whether animal or human, using more-or-less the same compositions of our earth chemical elements and water. For human babies, I recall a TV program years ago, revealing an unforgettable awareness to a younger me, that Our Creator stored much of these initial, vital, baby forming nutrients in our ladies' "cute" butts. What young lad would ever forget those words, and of course, every girl has a perfect "tush." So, personally, I think Our Creator Daddy has "eyes!!!" And moreover, Our Creator is quite the initial Baby Doctor; He included "in" our Mom's mammary glands, a Happy Birthing Hour drink, a shot of antibodies that Siri referred to as Colostrum. Even Mom animals have Colostrum in their mammary glands during birthing.

What a complete Super Duper Creator Daddy that we are Blessed to have in our lives. Big difference is that we humans get to talk to Our Creator Daddy via our inner "small" voices, which we find recorded in His Word. What is so outwardly incredible to me personally, is how incredibly beautiful our human females are; especially, "my" Princess Granddaughter. Like appreciating a gorgeous flower, her beauty begs one to seek a deeper understanding of "such a miracle" from her Creator Daddy. Thus, according to handy Siri, that the study of flowers, or "Anthology," reveals that the life and multiplication of flowers is notably-familiar-and-similar, to the life and multiplication of humans. And of course, Our Creator's stated creation multiplication wish in Genesis, Chapter One.

With just a teaspoon of imagination, the study of flowers could easily remind oneself of the childhood story of Cinderella. And that storyline could easily be scripted into a New York City Broadway Play; such as, the Beauty and the Beast. If I recall correctly, I enjoyed it more than five times as I treated my family and all my nieces, nephews and friends when they visited NYC. I never grew tired of Broadway "love stories" as they kindle the heart and can magically turn a Beast into a kneeling servant Prince. Neither did I grow tired of Broadway, or lately, my nearby St. Pete Mahaffey Theatre and their classic symphonies and sonatas. I always appreciate the tranquility offered this side of Heaven by the violins; however, this farm boy only understands the essence, or story behind the music, about as well as a Montana livestock auction.

And most definitely, my all-time favorite was Mamma Mia, which I enjoyed in London, Las Vegas, New York and even nearby in Tampa; plus, I have the home video available. I could enjoy that uplifting musical at least once or twice a year forever, and probably influenced by the fact that ABBA, a fellow Scandinavian group, provided the music. That "once or twice a year forever," would also include the video "Top Gun," should I "feel the need for speed!"

How wonderful it is that we get to tell Our Creator Daddy how beautiful His flowers are, and in my case, how beautiful my Granddaughter is; plus, all the Positive Love that Our Creator Daddy can sense within my Soul. Within that Siri overview study of flowers, I discovered that we men or males are essentially protector servants, and that my Granddaughter was right when she identified my Grampa role to be after all our family castle-like hierarchy lineup; yup, her servant. I am so Blessed to have that role in my very enriched, full life and enjoy it like an Oscar Award. And my final conclusion is that since my Granddaughter and all flowers are so outrightly beautiful; so, without a doubt, I believe that Our Creator Daddy has "eyes" for beauty as well.

If I remember correctly, I recall his joke, or as Joel Osteen says, "something funny," prior to his enlightening and very thorough messages praising Our Creator Father. Somewhat paraphrased to my literary need: Adam asked Our Creator Father, "Why did you make Eve so beautiful?" and Father replied, "So that you would like her." Then Adam asked, "Why does she do rather odd things, or seemingly less smart, like listening and talking to this serpent in our garden?" and Father replied, "So that she would like you." In my opinion, Joel Osteen is a superb, worldwide gifted purveyor of Our Creator Father's responses to Positive and negative choices, and all the explicit promises to be found throughout Our Creators' Word.

Regardless, we are all beautifully created, individually wrapped, including animals and creatures of the oceans, with mind boggling, functioning body parts, and of course, beauty features. According to Our Creator's Word, all we need to leave behind from old age, or from other reasons, is our physical bodies, which just assimilate back into mother earth. However, our human spiritual life as "in His or Our Creator's image," belongs to Our Creator Father. The ultimate question then becomes, do we grab this golden opportunity for eternal life alongside Our Creator Daddy, or literally take a "dirt" nap?

So, during my life storyline, where did my Bible study take me? For starters, get ready to read a run-on sentence about my inner voice from my childhood and that very same inner voice that I honor while sitting here typing away; that feeds me comforting thoughts as I compose. The very same inner "small" voice that feeds me Positive thoughts; that my, or anyone's imperfections are irrelevant to Our Creator Father. The very same inner "small" voice that informs me that Our Creator Father gave us "choice" during our creation, that we might "individually" recognize His Goodness, His Grace and His Love; then know, understand and witness His Positive Nature and

Power; that we should then Trust and become "one" with Our Creator Father and most important, once we know Jesus, Honor Our Creator by Honoring His Son. Then ideally, reciprocate His demeanor among all His creation, and/or all mankind by Honoring our Mathew 28 commission!!! From that planned run-on sentence, the natural byproduct is Positive Faith and a Ticket to the Eternal Life House.

And to me, that is not a religion, and need not be a religion. It is simply Our Creator's initial intention for all His mankind creation. It then becomes my obligation thereafter, if I proclaim to be the world's greatest fighter pilot, or more preferably, a great Dad and Granddad, I must step up and into the unknown, with the Faith of Daniel!!! Therefore, in Scene IV, I must and will muster enough of whatever to step into the whatever to begin an outreach website and "did so" in 2015. my neophyte game plan was and still ongoing, to reach into the unknown internet world; plus, social media world as a planet missionary and to begin a worldwide Honoring of Our Creator. That was another intentional run-on sentence. And then, my blog-a-book aspiration evolved from the thesis within my "About."

Actually, my aviation and sailing experiences have generated lots of kind people, telling me to write some sort of autobiography, or at least a log. I did log my sailing stops from our St. Pete home slip to BAR Harbor, Maine on scenic picture calendars from Arizona. Thank You, Jessica! Why Arizona? Because, Arizona beauty is the exact opposite of coastal beauty; and most of all, my eldest Son was born there and "there," my life became "Perfect." There I became Forever Grateful to Our Creator Father, AMEN!!!

But a bio? That did not interest me until I found this book in Barnes and Noble on "How to Blog a Book" by Nina Amir. How timely! Now I could work a worldwide internet website, integrate a worldwide twitter outreach and write about our Awesome Creator "Dad" around my Blessed life autobiography storyline. Seemed like a "win-win" to me and additionally, for the heritage awareness benefit to my precious Grandchildren. I shared my About to begin this book and in the Scene IV timeline, I expose "my About," written in 2015, to the world via Word Press. It summarizes and reinforces the directions for my intentions of this book. Teaser blogs were sent around the world via social media to find and invite all Our Creator's family members to share and Honor Our Common Daddy. Seemed simple and straight forward to me, but as I write this book, my website outreach still struggles to stir His worldwide family.

▸▸ Too Many Religions

I can understand why people reject religions and their mankind inflicted religious impacts on their lives, but no one should reject their Creator by rejecting their personal inner "small" voice. The only reason that I can understand if their religion becomes overly man oriented and dominates their daily life to the point that they reject the entire thesis of our creation. And that has catastrophic proportions: our entire Universe in my Opinion, is a Universe of Positives and negatives. An oversimplification of course, but in my Opinion, Our Creator uses this simple concept and arrangement to conduct His daily business and applies the Laws of Energy, maybe even $E=mc2$. Our Creator said in His Word, that nothing is impossible for Him, or what I like to hear, that all things are possible through Our Creator Daddy.

Throughout his Word, Our Creator implies that Positives, such as, Faith, Goodness, Grace, kind thoughts and most of all, Love, are the wishes in His Heart for all His Kids. Our Creator's Fatherly theme is "choice without condemnation." And if "we condemn ourselves," as in reject Him, or in my thinking, exude negative energy through our inner "small" voice, we are always welcome back regardless. Luke 15:11-32. These Gospel revelations are clearly featured in the oldest Book in His Word as well, and to me the book of insight, the Book of Job. The keys to His Fatherly Heart are our return of Positive love responses and accepted even in the size of a mustard seed. And of course, once you know His Name, then also Honor His Son Jesus with Positive appreciation of what Jesus endured on our behalf, Our Creator can provide around the clock awareness like an electrical security system. And most assuredly, for the unborn and all that have never heard of Jesus, or know his relevance, that they are covered under John 19:30. Regardless, none of that fear stuff that I recall from my youth. But once you know Jesus, any outward rejection of His Son, Jesus, is an outward rejection of Our Creator Father. In a world influenced by many energy forms, all governed by the Laws of Energy; yet, any rejections may put you into the negative energy world and by choice you may become muted in lay terms, or unnoticed in electrically natured energy terms.

But Good News, one Positive word that Honors Our Father or Jesus, you are back in the Positive energy realm and probably should sing the Hymn, Amazing Grace every day for the rest of your life. Plus, sing the Hymn, Blessed Assurance as I do and squeeze my Cross around my neck. I have no right to judge others; however, those two hymns are the big two in my life, and what I would like to hear from above at my celebration "wake." Plus, including any and all hymns sung by country singer, Allan Jackson. And another Air Force kid like my Super Sons.

Pastor Joel Osteen is a master at finding all the Positives wishes within Our Creator's Word, that will surely benefit the lives of all His Kids or His mankind creation. The many times that I read our Creator's Word during those long flights, the more I began to pick up on Our Creator's desire and/or intent to come visit His creation. Much of Our Creator's composition was about daily issues, daily lives stuff and lots of family-tree begets to set the history time line. However, within His Word, from Genesis to His Prophets, Our Creator included within His plan, to come visit His earthly family and He "did" just that. Like so many before me and now old news, I perceived a pathway of intent through Isaiah and

Zechariah. Then Hallelujah, now just slightly over 2000 years ago, around the world, we respectfully look forward to each Christmas season to celebrate Our Creator and the Birth of His Son Jesus!!! And guess what, the Donkey was there and the trail of the Donkey continues!!!

I satisfied my Bible study needs for the moment during the latter days in Scene III. Taking a few life hints from the Buddhist religion, I took their word "nirvana" or inner contentment, and when applied, quickly noted that my life overflowed with internalized, obvious Blessings. Only difference, I credited Our Creator, Our very same "Daddy!!!" Comments from our astronauts regarding their perceptions of Our Creator and His Universe, had magically internalized an excitement to see Our Creator Father in a totally new light. my dots to understanding Our Creator began to stretch the word spirit into spiritual power, and in order to create all that "is," then into spiritual energy power. Therefore, the obvious resulting conclusion for me, then becomes that Our Creator Father is thee "Spiritual Energy Entity," who manages (present tense) everything created within our Universe for starters. Amen!!! However, and I repeat, Our Creator Father did not create religions, man did!!!

my Scene III, or Airline Era, came to an end by a FAA regulation that said I must discontinue flying as an airline pilot by age 60. It has since been changed to 65, but nevertheless, I enjoyed my retirement flight to Zurich, Switzerland in a brand-new B-767, still with the smell of a new car. That was on April 9, 2001, and on my Grandpa Lars' birthday, an immigrant from Norway. Proudly, I am his third American generation. my youngest Son, his fourth generation, had accomplished getting his private flying license and was authorized by the chief pilot to ride in the cockpit jump seat, right behind me, or Dad. A few more instruments than his Cessna 172. I was most grateful to my airline for wonderfully treating my family to first class seating as well. I proudly watched my eldest Son, using the nighttime flight across the "pond" to Europe, to continue studying his demanding law school books. And sitting in 1A, next to my Alpha Tau Omega Son in 2A, was Miss "Tri-Delta." In countless ways, a Perfect "Catch-of-a-Lifetime" for my Perfect Son. So Perfect, that Mom and I had already adopted her back in 1996, after meeting Miss Florida for the first time at my Son's frat party. Mom was a definite Eleven on a scale of one to ten, but Miss Florida was also graced with southern magnetism and sweetener, so a definitive Twelve.

For me as Dad, "Tri" meant "Triple" Super Lady, or Super Stunning, Super Sweet and of course, Super Gator Smart. This super Blessed Dad felt very proud to have my full family on board and most grateful to my airline as well. Especially appreciative to my Sweetheart for making up balloons, napkins, signs and special cards for all passengers; that all would be included and honor this special occasion. my airline added to the party ambiance with free champagne and cake for all passengers.

The following year, the lucky frat kid and the sorority girl were married in a classic small chapel, only to have a huge beach party celebration. Over seventy cases of beer, champagne and wine should adequately enable an approximation of "huge." And now for the Gramma and Grampa latest headlines: After a few years of recovering from-that-one-of-a-kind beach party, we now have Three Amazing and Awesome Blessings that literally made "my" Life "Complete!!!" Amen!!! I would normally save those adjectives just for Our Creator "Daddy," but since He is a Grampa Himself, countless times over, I know that He will totally understand!!!

NEWARK... NEW YORK'S MOST CONVENIENT AIRPORT

NEW YORK

Continental
Airlines

SCENE

IV

Armageddon???????

But that year, 2001, the USA felt the first taste of Armageddon and with the biblical touches by some of the expected players and for some of their misguided reasons; yet, prewarned in the last chapter in Our Creator's Word. Though not where expected, but in downtown New York City near Wall Street, the World Trade Center. A place where I used to occasionally chill out in a Borders book store; then catch the subway below to somewhere around New York, or the PATH Train back to our crew pad in Newark. During the unexpected attack, they were probably yelling, "Allah is great," or their "god." Yes, a man-made religion; and as I stated above or earlier, could not be the actions of Our Creator. What creator father would destroy; as creator's create, not destroy.

Muhammad, a caravan trader, got the blame; however, he was illiterate and could not read nor write according to Siri. But a man or men did write the Koran and used certain words that could easily be misconstrued; and behold, another man did lead malleable minds to misguided outcomes in the name of religion. Thus, Siri showed that 2977 people perished in minutes and a haunting resemblance of an attempted step toward Armageddon. So, the question arises: How did Our Creator handle this situation? If it was the result of an Armageddon-like event; then as dramatically described in Our Creator's Word, and in His Revelation's Chapter Three, is Our Creator Father's Promise of a split-second Rapture for all believers. His Super Son, Jesus, confirmed in His Gospels, that Belief, Acceptance, Faith, Trust, or any Positive Spirit inclinations would connect with Our Creator Father, "even if" in the size of a "mustard seed," and would be all that is needed to be included.

As eluded above, my takeaway thinking is that Our Creator is a "Spiritual 'Energy' Entity" that can make things happen the very same way that He created all that "is" In His' "In the Beginning", and can, or will honor our belief and bring us home to eternal spiritual life with Him, using the very same spiritual energy that created everything "In the Beginning."

That sentence was another run-on, because Our Creator is a run-on sort of Father, who can deliver Split-Second results through His means and ways as a "Spiritual Energy Entity," and faster than I can type. And I repeat, logic says that it's the very same energy used by Our Creator during His "In the Beginning!!!" Thus, Honoring Our Creator in terms of energy need not be mystical, nor interpreted or explained in a religion context. Our Creator Father is simply the Singular Mastermind of all that "is!" And He did not create religions, man did!!!

This perception became more apparent over the years as I studied the Laws of Energy, the Laws of Nature, and then noted that our Universe thrives on Positives and negatives within the energy laws. These perceptions were not so much from what the scientists said and recorded, but more what they did not say. Nor what theologians say, but again, what they did, or do not say. To fully understand the Universe equation of Positives and negatives is the basic grade school awareness that Positives and negatives attract, but likes repel. In other words, Our Creator Father, Mr. Positive, needs to work by Himself. The planets are essentially negative and well separated, so no repelling nor sparking;

thus, the Universe and its Galaxies are seemingly in agreement for Our "One" Creator Father to do His thing. And the beauty of it all, His thing as in "energy thing," underlies a similar understanding of our mankind successes with the conceptualization and functionality of both the internet and its sidekick, the iCloud. And that energy thing is an "electrical" energy thing and "invisible" until it's activated or requested by some means.

Our Creator Father's "energy thing" or His "potential response capability thing" is conceptually and functionally the same and always there to support our "911" calls from our inner "small" voices. Yup, I keep taking and sending pictures of my Grandchildren to my iPhone, or off to storage in my iCloud. With just a tap on my iPhone, that activates a binary electrical pulse and off to my iPhone, or my iCloud, another picture among my latest count of over 7000. And I "can bring back," any or all, in a flash. Surely sounds like what we expect by Faith that Our Creator Daddy "can or will do" as well. Such as in an accident, or any demise with a lighting-like flash of Positive energy, and with the pulse amperage of a "mustard seed," or whatever is needed. Yup, I totally believe that Our Creator Daddy "can bring back" home to His House, any Positive Soul in a flash as well!!!

For our iPhones to retrieve, or to send or demand a requested picture to or from iCloud via its associated electrical system, it needs an around-the-clock, charged or stored internal exciter voltage, or a capacitance of stored energy, to respond in a binary blink of an eye. And guess what, Our Creator Daddy designed our bodies with a similar stored energy-like capacitance within our body neural system, that He could and would recognize, or sense in terms of a Faith or Trust-like energy, or any Positive nature energy emitting from our inner "small" voice. Then respond in a split-second for all those that need His flash binary ride to Our Creator Daddy's i-Heaven. Or just to answer Positive Prayer and requests from His kids who need His Creator's touch, like the kids in St. Jude's care, or the Shriners' Hospital care. All these kids have owned a piece of my heart for a very long time, and most assuredly have a direct connection to their Creator Daddy!!!

The tangible and visible fascination for me now as a Grampa, having been initially raised without electricity, and now have visually watched mankind operating and working from their orbiting space station, is that Our Creator Daddy also has provided His mankind the necessary intelligence to also work with the intangible and the invisible wireless freedoms within my lifetime. The "in His Image," intelligence factor is clearly tied to electrically natured energy and/or the Universe of Positives and negatives that His mankind creation can sense, send or return electrically through our inner "small" voice. Thank goodness, that Our Creator installed our electrically natured circuitry, it also makes us do the right thing when you see a grizzly bear or a rattlesnake; unless of course, you have the cool Faith of Daniel. So, what's next? And from where does Siri do her thing? And since she knows everything, who taught her, Our Creator Daddy?

As I departed my airline era, these thoughts that Our Creator Father was a "Spiritual Energy Entity," had not yet been personally, nor mentally cultured to a pearly-white level. They were set aside during my quest to discover new flying opportunities. Back when I flew the Lear 24, then generally used by the famed Johnny Carson, a nighttime TV program host, I also got a Learjet rating as well as my Airline Transport Rating. Thus, I felt comfortably qualified about my airline follow-on flying endeavors. However, the air ambulance company that wanted to hire me for my Lear aircraft rating and my world-wide level experience, had instead cut back and went broke as a result of the "nine-eleven world trade center" event.

With a "hang loose" mindset and as a retirement hobby, I turned to my O'Day 27 sailboat and decided to make it livable and self-sustaining. I used every local boat show to "steal" thoughts about making the Nurse T & Skipper Me as cozy; as user friendly and comfortable as the million-dollar boats. Even concocted a king size bed arrangement in the salon area; with nighttime potty needs a step away. Also added a TV with DVD movie capabilities, and of course, popcorn and bar desires, also a step away.

In reality, our O'Day was better suited for my quest because with its draft; we could go places those other rather expensive, higher draft boats could not go, like anywhere around the north side of the Florida Keys. Thus, in 2010, we tested my tinkering and enjoyed the Keys for five months and observed numerous wine-flavored, "green flash" sunsets—sounds like visual Blessings to me.

The thought of one day, sailing it from St Pete to Maine, actually started as I would often depart my airline base in Newark, New Jersey for either Florida or South America. When en route, I would think about the feasibility and the "how of doing just that." Well, as I compose this book, I can confirm that on April 18, 2010, my Sweetheart and I departed the St Pete area, enjoyed my April birthday on Cabbage Key island for an entire week, passed the USA most southern point in the Florida Keys; and did arrive in Kittery, Maine on July 12, 2017. Cabbage Key is only available by boat, and where, I was told, Jimmy Buffet wrote his hit song: "Cheeseburger in Paradise." There we invested a few bucks on the walls and ceiling of their unique restaurant, and I bought one of my favorite t-shirts. On it said, "all who wonder are not lost." That certainly covers my world travel quests and my resulting Blessings.

I will add occasional bits from this superb experience as my storyline continues through this time era. But during my "hang loose" time after my airline days, I received a call from a young lad that had the aviation bug from his youth and had become an accomplished pilot the hard way. He was super likeable and was also super diligent; thus, he was selected to be the Chief Pilot for a fractional ownership upstart. He had earned his stripes and credentials while flying for the aforementioned, now the defunct air ambulance company.

The odd part of all this was the aircraft that I would be flying. Ever heard of a Piaggio 180, an aircraft with two engines and with its props in the "rear;" plus, a canard on its nose. Made in Italy by a motor scooter company. Really? What an odd-looking flying machine! For me, with fifteen aircraft types and sizes under my belt of experience, this number sixteen, odd-goose airplane was a pleasant surprise for me. I recall once at 39,000 feet heading east, with a jet-stream tailwind and noticing that this "prop" job was doing over 500 knots ground speed. What I enjoyed about this aircraft and its mission, was that it normally included a "dead head" leg, or no passengers and a chance to enjoy "freedom" flying. It offered me, a retired Air Force Fighter Pilot, opportunities such as cancelling IFR, or instrument flight rules and flying visual flight rules, or VFR, like an eagle around the Bahama Islands, the Rocky Mountains, the Cascade Mountains chain of volcanoes, and especially the Cabo San Lucas area looking for whales. However, my forever memories, will be the hugs after each flight with everyone's favorite girl on the TV show "Laugh In," Madam Goldie Hawn. What a Blessing to top off my aviation career!!! So, to the young lad, then the chief pilot who hired me, thank you, Chad. And Kurt, a pilot as well and a super actor, I did notice you; especially, in my favorite western movie, Tombstone! And who could ever forget your filmed together movie, Overboard, and that cold water scene. Brrrrrrr!

Wrapping up my aviation career, it all started with props in front, then jets both small and later, three or four engines big, and ending with props in the rear. That pusher prop engine concept seems poetic when you factored in my ever-so-subtle aging. Flying requires the art of navigation and so does boating. Thus, I moved on from 5-600 hundred knots to 5-6 Knots; again, seemingly poetic. However, a trained navigation mindset can be cross-handy regardless, and translates well should you need to apply similar thinking. When using maps, there is a correlation; but when boating, my favorite navigation back up is looking for "local knowledge" aids, or other boaters. At 5-6 knots, one has time to analyze the situation to see if it's heading toward the locally desired "Happy Hour" marina.

There were several with fun memories galore, but our family loaded week vacation in and around the Boston Harbor in 2017, takes the honor. The Grandkids got to sleep on the boat with a rock star "parking" boat slip at the Boston Waterboard Marina, while their Mom and Dad enjoyed the next-door Marriott Hotel at the Long Wharf. The Boston Harbor, with so much history, offered family orientated whale watching, get-wet speed boat runs and even close by, were rides on the subway over to the Boston Red Sox Fenway Park for an evening game with the Minnesota Twins. Previously mentioned, another keeper memory for me, occurred at that mom-and-pop marina just north of Hilton Head. So classically southern, we tied up to a rickety old marina and right behind a classic shrimp boat. A forever Air Force friend, Jessica's Dad, was with me at the time and we enjoyed an ageless southern setting with a pot of boiling water, filled with corn cobs and fresh shrimp from the classic shrimp boat on our bow. Paradises come in so many flavors and that was truly one of a kind—never to be forgotten; not to mention the thick, unforgettable deep south brogue dialect.

All of my East-Coast sailing stops seemed to mingle with history, and let me live and walk through my childhood history books and classes en route to a Happy Hour in "very" old buildings like Hemmingway's in Beaufort, S.C. or the Back Street Pub in Beaufort, N.C. Most memorable from my childhood history awareness was all our country forming activity throughout the Chesapeake and the Delaware area. Most history-book notables were the marina stops in St Augustine, Florida, Norfolk, near Jamestown, Virginia and Plymouth Rock, Massachusetts. As to who "really" discovered America, since according to Siri, Columbus never quite made it. Well, a policeman in Plymouth Rock told me, "St Augustine."

Boating, whether in open waters or via the inner coastal waterways, does keep one's mind expectedly wrapped around what you "cannot" see. Running aground in the Florida waters is generally a sandbar, but beyond southern waters, it is generally rocks, that play for keeps and "own" lots of boats. This fact was made very clear in the Carolina's and continued North to Maine. Sailing around the Carolina's demanded lots of attention to map detail. But as expected, added tons of fond memories from the waterway bookends, from the southern Beaufort to the northern Beaufort. Also, where my fellow Co-Grampa joined me near Cape Fear and took a sea level break from his demanding, no happy hour watering holes available, hiking trip up the Appalachian Trail. Thus, so proud of his old football coach grit and respectful of his entire trail accomplishment.

Although not planned, both Grandpas reached their most northern destinations in Maine the very same year or 2019—one by foot; the other by sailboat. But in Maine, if by sail, it would be more correct to call it "Down East." What an example of "just do it" for our treasured Grandsons.

And where my Montana cattle rancher brother-in-law joined me for a break from his demanding haying season back in Montana. The northern Beaufort marina and its history with pirates, only embellished our Happy Hour times. With their super Carolina country singers as well and with choices of several waterfront parties to enjoy; yup, another treasure trove of memories. While there, my brother-in-law and I were honored to have a tour of the eye-catching boat, the "SanBob," owned by family acquaintances. So big, it needed an outside slip and it lit up like a Christmas tree at night. It probably cost a half herd of cows and their calves, but we were so impressed of all the places to store cases of Bud Lite—priorities when out fishing, and in this case, Marlin.

After departing from Beaufort North, took my brother-in-law to Bern, North Carolina, to catch a flight back to Montana. There, we discovered that Bern was the birthplace of Pepsi, my favorite, by a local pharmacist. From Bern, now departing solo and continuing northbound toward Norfolk for Winter drydock storage, I was always puzzled by the name of the next town in North Carolina called "Oriental." Well, you guessed it, according to the locals, there is a sunken Chinese ship nearby. During my sailing years up the coast, I encountered several popup storms that challenged my resolve. The day I departed a fun stop in Oriental on a nice, sunny morning, on an easterly heading in Pamlico Sound, and would be turning northernly after two or three more markers. Then off my port side, what appeared to be just a nice day, traveling north to south, deck washing rain showers; then yup, one of those misread, memorable popup's hit me on the port side. Normally, turning and keeping the bow into the storm takes care of the challenge, but that would put me heading toward land and mostly likely one of those North Carolina boat-collecting rocks. Expectedly, my visibility went to zero in a flash, So in these unfamiliar waters, fresh with the Chinese ship story on my mind, I turned to put the storm on my stern and open waters. Not fun! I had given myself a hard-to-manage, broaching situation and a forever lasting memory of the Carolina seemingly kind waters. That similar scenario hit me again in Delaware Bay, but this time the popup storm, also from the northwest, hit me from the stern. my course to Lewes, Delaware was southeast, so I kept my scary, uncomfortable and potentially broaching course. That day and that storm, the wave frequency was such that I was almost able to surf ride the wave tops. It was wearing, but workable and another memory.

However, looking back, my scariest storm encounter, was during an anchor night back in Mosquito Bay near Cape Canaveral. A front was reported by the news, but we always have those in Florida, so no big concern. During my sailing years, I was late to the game in my understanding of winds in general. Winds were important as well during my aviation years, but were factored in mostly for landing and fuel considerations. For sailing, the winds are perceived complementary, even necessary and also indicative where the fronts are coming from. Living in Florida, one begins to note quickly that winds initially blow toward impending fronts and hurricanes, or a high to a low. More concerned about passing grades on crosswind landings, I missed that fact during my Air Force pilot training classes on weather. And now that my boat, the Nurse T & Skipper Me is in Maine, the famed Nor'easters term finally became understandable as to their attention getting, destructive potential. The wind blows from the Northeast high pressure, but the problem weather actually comes into the area from the Southwest low pressure—I missed that understanding in my weather class. This past summer, a tropical storm over Texas eventually continued up to Maine and kept re-defining the word Nor'easter for me, for several days.

One more thing, before I leave this discourse involving Maine, that I found odd to grasp. When I left Florida to sail to Maine, I always had a mindset that I would generally see a Northernly heading on the compass. But no, after Portland, I thought I was having compass issues, as it was always pointing EAST. In my mind, I should be sailing northerly to Bar Harbor, but my Sweetheart and I went so far East that I began to expect to see signs to Norway. In Maine, it is referred to as "Down East," but it just seemed odd to go East to get to northern Maine. Fortunately for this full-blooded Norwegian, my Navionics App in my iPad knew the way better than I.

Anyway, back to my anchor night in Mosquito Bay and in clear sight of the Cape Canaveral launch pad, the bow was facing southeast toward the high-pressure area, or the initial wind direction; then as the storm rains' became noticeable, the boat suddenly swung around to the northwest. Through my plexiglass side windows and hatch cover, the lightning lit up the area, so I mentally prepped for a mast strike and kept myself on top of a bunk foam mattress. I heard once that Florida is the lightning capital of the world, so prior to launching, I had hooked up heavy gage copper wires to the mast shroud wires, to be dropped into the water during storms or lightning in the area. my goal was to give lightning a circuit back into the water and hopefully prevent onboard lightning impacts or worse, bodily harm.

On the bow, I had my onboard dinghy hooked to a gib halyard, but not tied down. I did that, so, if the sail boat sank for whatever reason, the dinghy would float up and off, yet tied to the thirty-five-foot mast by another thirty-five foot, or longer, halyard. That would cover most of the water depth, that I would encounter up the coast.

As I looked out through the transparent hatch, I watched my dinghy literally flying around my mast; then eventually landing on top of the rear Bimini. The next morning, the TV local weather channel, was reporting 90-mph winds along the front that had passed over the Cape Canaveral area during the night. Another unforgettable experience on the "high seas." And yes, after that sudden directional spin, I sat inside with my safety vest on. And yes, after each encounter with weather on the "high seas," I so admire all sailors of the yesteryears.

Bottom line, finding time to "only" think about Our Creator Father was not quite as incidental to the expected tranquility time that one might expect when sailing. As the mind wonders over the Majesty of His creations, so does the bow of the boat and the need for continual awareness; especially in the Intercoastal Waterways, or ICW. In these situations; however, either on the waters or above in the skies, so many opportunities to let my inner voice Honor Our Creator and also visually honoring His creation. And during those moments, like Jesus in His 40 days of isolation with the Father, new understandings start to evolve. As I would honor my inner "small" voice and just listen, a calming, internalized clarification of the means and ways of Our Creator became and still becomes humanly transparent and understandable. The "means" as in meaning His Spirit and His command; the "ways" or His energy connection to accomplish the entire Creation itself. Then tying Our Creator's nature into what creators do and not do, or connecting the dots from a Spirit Entity to an Energy Entity as well. Then noting from my life awareness that life within our Universe and probably beyond as well, is a realm of Positives and negatives. So vast, that I can only handle this thinking at the "lay" level, or "Siri" level in my case.

So, what did I just propose? Well, in my humble Opinion, Our Creator Father can only do good or Positive responses, like you would expect from a true father figure, JOB 34:10. But a negative in whatever form is equally necessary as well. Sort of like a universe size battery with the planets acting as the largely inert, negative poles for lack of a better word. We humans are largely negative as well; thus, lightning strike prone. However, we also have our saving grace feature as "in His image," or our "inner 'small' voice." And if we honor Our Creator Father with Positive Faith and Trust, we can, by His Word, then count on split-second rescue from lightning, or car accidents, or any rapture event, requiring Our Creator's instant intervention, and so covered in verse 2 of the Hymn "Blessed Assurance".

The stars and our sun, a star as well, are celestial like planets, but with nuclear fusion capability, capable of producing light. That sounds like Our Creator Father stating that He "is" the Spiritual Energy Source, who lit the match, causing the Universe to light up via hydrogen/helium nuclear fusion on the first day of His creation. Thank You, Father!!! From the moment as a young boy who lost his "bag of pennies" and now approaching my eighties, my perception that Our Creator Father is a Super Amazing, Awesome Father Figure, totally infallible, provable true as I AM WHO I Am, and even outwardly, "notary stamped" true as He clearly stated in His Word! Amen!!! So, it's time to bring the Donkey on stage for the rest of the book and present a much belated recognition. However, that is often the normal life of a "servant" figure.

▸▸ Enter the Donkey

For the curious and quick readers, the Donkey, to whom I have dedicated this book, now enters the picture hereafter. Siri said the Donkey is mentioned 142 times in Our Creator's Word and four times in the Quran. The Donkey is looked upon like a servant slave animal and gets lots of abuse as a result. However,

I surmise that the Donkey was created and planted among Our Creator's kids for a specific reason. That reason is that a typical Donkey is "in horse talk," only about seven hands or less. They are generally very docile and amicable around people; plus, a perfect evolutionary, subservient natured animal to subtly authenticate and notarize Our Creator's Word right under His kids or people's noses. So, in my book, the Donkey will get its long-awaited claim to fame and "top billing!!!" The reason: The Donkey was part of all prophecies regarding Mother Mary, Thee Messiah, or Our Creator's Son, JESUS. And on its back, Our Creator had created an IMPRINT of a CROSS!!!

Guess where and when we, mankind saw that again? Now Forever IMPRINTED in our Minds, our Hearts and our Souls!!! Hmmm, how did that get missed? Most likely because Donkeys sort of get unnoticed until needed. Sort of like an Uber driver servant, and sort of like my Princess Granddaughter's Grandpa, her lucky servant. And that's me! Like so many children's books and their stories, her Daddy is the King, her Mommy is the Queen, her Brothers are both Princes and her Gramma is a Queen as well. Only one family role available, was to be her Servant; and as expressed earlier within this book, I feel internally super Blessed to be in that role around my Princess. And I am over-compensated with lots of cute winks and my singular privilege to kiss Her hand anytime I say "May I." Until she goes to college and needs a car, I am really valuable. I wonder if she would like to drive Grandpa's Corvette, which would then be over 30 years old.

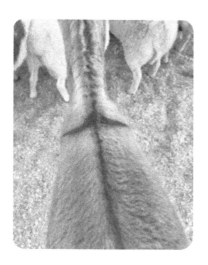 

Now over 2000 years ago, we still see the CROSS, thee SIGNATURE symbol of Our Creator, and in my Opinion. His PREPLANNED scripted course for His Son, Jesus. During my worldwide travels, I noted the Cross nearly everywhere around the world; plus, like me, proudly wearing the Cross on a chain around my neck during those travels. Again, Our Creator did "not" create religions, is "not" a religion, need "not" be a religion. Moreover, Our Creator's Word is a standalone Document and should "not" be a religion in itself either. May I remind and repeat, that the Donkey was created well prior to Our Creator's Word, then included in His Word as an intentionally created, explicit "outward" evidence that Our Creator is a "very real" Entity. And then sets the timeline to corroborate that Our Creator's Word was tied to the Egyptian Papyrus era, and tied to the spiritual needs and relationship with the enslaved family lineage of Abraham, or the chosen Jewish nation. As a summary or repeat of my assessment or Opinion, the Donkey "is" part of Our Creator's Word, and the Donkey "is" Our Creator's symbolism of a humble servant and carries Our Creator's favorite symbol of a perfect "Cross" on its back. Thereby, subtly authenticating all messages within His WORD; that we should expect Our Creator to become visible among us and HE DID!!! AMEN!!!

Religions were probably inevitable when considering all evolutionary aspects, including languages, communications, recording means, etc. But religions should and could become a thing of the past in "respect" to Our "Common Daddy." Insidious politics, regardless if religion based or not, gradually inflict cult biases. It's totally understandable how they originated, but are they necessary? No doubt that Jesus will do away with religions on his Second Coming. He will probably reiterate that Our Creator "Daddy" created everyone with interchangeable parts and we all bleed red. Thus, simply no reason not to have around-the-world, mutual Common "Daddy" respect and family harmony. And my endeavor wish till then is to foster a common ground, common sense worldwide peace theme through this book and my Matthew 28 website!!!

If one is in peace with Our Common Creator, then why the Armageddon-like attack on the NYC World trade center on 9/11/2001. Of all the religions to have committed such an atrocity, why Islam? Their timeless greeting is "peace be upon you," and one normally responds in the same manner, or better. During my Air Force Era, I always found Muslims to be very congenial and compatible; although my relationships were primarily with aviator camaraderie overtones. During my Airline Era, it was rather common to party at the Gatwick Hilton Hotel bar with the Iranians as they were the most compatible, westernized people in the Mideast. During my Air Force Era, I found that the Iranians sure loved to spend the Shah's money and party, that the Saudi's all wanted to be treated like Kings, and that the Jordanians were simply nice and transparent, like North Dakota farm kids. At the time, I did not get to meet any Egyptians until the eve of Y2K. and what a nice surprise!!!

An immigrant from the Egypt Nasser era and a former air force pilot just like me; actually, a former Russian Mig pilot no less, and now crewed with a former F-4 driver—a perfect crew combination for our flight departing from NYC to Florida on the eve of 12/31/1999. But, I must admit that when I saw an "Arab" sitting in the Copilot seat, I probably thought something like "why me Lord?" However, that thought was totally momentary as my Creator Father most assuredly knew that I would be the perfect common host aviator for the situation. Our common pilot rhetoric quickly set the tone of teamwork for the somewhat odd occasion, end of story. We had the best time comparing old notes. I do not recall the word religion ever coming up. All pilots regardless of who they are, or where they are from, are Positive type people and so is Our Creator. Thus, most pilots keep Our Creator Daddy close to our vest everywhere we fly and go anyway. So, we cut to the chase and talked about girls and airplanes in no particular order, or typical pilot talk. Since we were both married with kids in colleges, we quickly switched to cockpit talk like what first class dinners were available and our crew hotel located on the beach. Plus, my Sweetheart joined me for a New Year Eve night on the town in Fort Lauderdale. We were flying a rather new B-757, which without a doubt, the closest airline airplane to a fighter aircraft, so a very enjoyable Y2K experience.

Then into a new century, and soon to become new headlines of an unexpected evil, some very rich Muslim kids begun under the radar; like bugs under a rug and probably for some time, wanting to impress his, or their "Allah," by blowing the socks off a normally peaceful man-made religion by mixing it with man-made political aspirations. With too much money available and too much desire for fame, it festered into a super dangerous terrorist faction. Thus, discoloring the Islam flag, and insulting the Islam religion. The reason given: Destroy the "infidels." Only mentioned one time in the Quran and in Surah 9:5, but what became an explosive banner to commit terror; supposedly to honor their Allah, their word for God. The world was on its toes and ready for Y2K, but not an attack by Muslims kids taking pilot training within the USA, as that was considered normal. During my Air Force era, I had been a T-38 Flight Instructor for several very nice mid-east kids. However, this roque group cleverly planned and orchestrated the unexpected, the around-the-world shattering news, the 9/11/2001 attack on the NYC World Trade Center. Big problem kids, Creator's create; not destroy, so forget the virgins.

What the Quran actually says about nonbelievers is that they are rejectors of faith, and is rather close to my thinking. I sense that their pattern of thinking stemmed from historical awareness and affiliation with Jesus, whom the Islam writers credited as a prophet. my thinking of Our Creator and His how, HIS means and His ways to run His Universe, is in terms of Positives and negatives as well; although I connect Energy relationships to Positives and negatives, which explains Our Creator's "In The Beginning" and His daily management means of all that is visible, or invisible and all that is tangible, or intangible. Since I fully believe that Our Creator conducts His Universe intra-action from a Spiritual Positive Energy Entity influence; then such synonyms as Accept, or reject; Belief, or reject; Faith, or reject; Hope, or reject; and of course, Love, or hate, all have Positive relevance, or negative life outcomes and consequences. Most importantly, is that I fully believe that Our Creator Daddy can only do POSITIVE GOOD, as Creator's create, and any Positive perception by Our Creator in the size of Mustard Seed will provide a First-Class ticket back to Our Creator's Spiritual Heaven, should that need ever arise. And that "is" the message that JESUS assured everyone in His Gospels and Outwardly guaranteed and SIGNED VISUALLY on the CROSS!!! And of course, Pre-authenticated and Pre-notarized His Gospel Contract, John 19:30, by the CROSS on the Donkey's back, and intended as such from the moment the Donkey was created.

How Our Creator conducts his Father Figure role, seemingly corresponds with Islam, or simply about their Allah's conduct regarding believers and nonbelievers. But then the Quran gets thick with qualifiers. And then, back to my starting point is Our Creator's Word, that Our Creator Father did not create religions. The Islam religion was birthed by mankind, (570-632), for their area communal reasons; thus, Islam evolved much later than Judaism and Christianity. The Islam religion is highly influenced by major players from and within Our Creator's Word and it's almost a family affair; namely Abraham's son,

Ishmael as the heritage parent of Islam. Mother Mary and JESUS, are honored in Surah Three, so Islam had its chance to evolve into a near-family religion of believers, but misunderstood wording written during the Mohammod era, seemingly causes considerable confusion within the religion itself. First, the Quran is loaded with conduct-tripping rules, thus, prompting impromptu choices by rogue followers, to justify ulterior motives outside the Quran and then judge to their self-serving agenda. Rogue Islam leaders with too much money, redefined the word "Kafir" to the social platform messages of our time; very much like the Pharisees during the time of Jesus. Suddenly we, or the rest of the world, are all "infidels." The Kafir souls are considered the "ungrateful" and/or maybe "rejectors of faith." Siri said that Islam teaches a final judgement with the righteous "rewarded in paradise and unrighteous punished in hell."

That theme generally corresponds and collaborates with existing religions, suggesting that it has been influenced by lots of interchange of inner "small" voices over the years. Thus, it appears that all or most of Our Creator's kids are on the same page, but several seem not sure who is influencing their inner "small" voices and just follow the money.

This is where Faith steps in to Honor their Inner "small" Voice and To Honor Our Creator. While on our honeymoon in 1971, in Mexico City and then later onto Acapulco, my Sweetheart and I toured the famed Metropolitan Cathedral in the middle of Mexico City. We witnessed and visualized "Faith" in action as people crawled on their hands and knees for several blocks and possibly further, on cobble stones no less, and on into the Cathedral—never to be a forgotten visual image of FAITH itself! Although no dangers were present, that was an outward demo of the "Faith of Daniel," that I will never forget. Now 49 years later, I will present the "how" and the "means" that Our Creator Common Daddy will use, in my Opinion, to answer their Positive beliefs or negative responses.

As I write this page, the coronavirus is the world headline, and attacking the world population. This virus does not discriminate and most assuredly demonstrates that we all have the same Daddy. Our Creator's living human population, and their age-old religions and their politics unfortunately discriminate. For those who may wonder why I did not, or have not and will not consider people races and their religions. Simple, Our Creator created all people with one common "internal" soul "in His image." And personally, I have yet to find a race that I did not like, and nor a race that I like better. Regardless of race, I have found a handshake and a hug and you quickly become a team for Our Creator Father. But with religions and politics, not so much. We all have gifts from Our Creator Daddy to make a happy family, regardless of race.

If we need a religion, let's call it a world religion of Positives, or the opposite, a religion of negatives. Understanding Our Creator Father in terms of a Spiritual "Energy" Entity, a religion of Positives would be compatible. Our Creator, a Positive Energy Entity, can react with all those with a Positive Belief, or Faith in Our Creator Daddy, and all those who follow the religion of negatives, or the rejectors, are always welcome. As I eluded to earlier, I prefer to use the word "rejector" rather than sinner. The use of the word "sinner" is often used as a blanket word and may then appear to the self-righteous to include the Unborn and/or all those whom were never exposed to Our Creator's Word, or who have never heard of His Son, Jesus. Jesus clarified that all His people or His church, (people or church, same meaning), past, present and future, only need to bring to the table is

Faith the size of a "mustard seed," and for all those before Jesus, or who never heard of Jesus, the very same Faith in the Great White Buffalo to Honor Our Creator has all the "Positive" power recognition that Our Creator Father requires to perform His Spiritual Energy thing! Works not required! Amen!!! All of Father's "prodigal" family members are welcome without judgement, and as I stated earlier, "choice without condemnation" is Our Father's choice and theme throughout His Word. my hero, His wonderful Son Jesus, confirmed that in John 3:16, and again in John 19:30. Then both the Donkey, whom Jesus rode to this event, and then on a highly honored Friday, still to this day, Jesus validated this Blessed Assurance event, set up by our Creator Father and became my favorite hymn as well. First, when the Donkey, a prophetic humble "servant" symbol, who was created with a vivid Cross "stamped" on its back, and then eventually when Jesus vividly "signed" our assurance upon the everlasting Cross. More to follow, but for now, sounds like a "notary stamped and signed" contract with Our Creator "Daddy's" new "unveiled" open door policy to me. The "Laws of Moses" were simplified to "Love your Daddy and Love your Neighbor!!!" We owe Jesus a debt of gratitude for His CliffsNotes to His Father's

Word in Matthew 22:36-40? How can something that simple become a religion? Only if twisted by man-made political motives to the eventual detriment of Our Creator "Daddy."

⤷ **Bucket List Cruise Around the World.**

With my aviation years under my belt and my sloop, the Nurse T & Skipper Me, sailing years now underway as well, what better way than to let my bucket list run-eth over with 110-day cruise around the world. And let professionals fill some remaining curiosities about our incredible world. my Sweetheart wanted to see the Panama Canal and walk the wall in China. Personally, I just love to wander, to feel the blessings of "all who wander are not lost" and enjoy one Happy Hour after another. Anyway, "it's all good Dad," as my youngest Son would often tell me—mostly, after he wanted to change the subject of some fatherly discussion.

Feeling reasonably well healed after retiring from the airlines, we still had to "sell the farm" to pay for this lengthy cruise, but it was worth every penny. I found the entire cruise to be awesome; that could be an entire book in itself. From my military and airline years, I was familiar with much of our major stops, but so notable was the precision management of the Panama Canal, walking around Easter Island, wondering about stupid stuff like why the cows around me did not fall off the earth, since they were upside down from the cows in my childhood era back in North Dakota, And now here, mid Pacific, west of South America and east of Australia, and now walking around the monumental statues or the "moai." But once again avoiding stepping in cow paddies, the very same thing I did as a kid, but now upside down.

We were not allowed on Pitcairn Island, our next stop, but now own some of their wood mementos. Tahiti is a must stop of course, to fill the romantic island square; then seven stops in New Zealand, taking note of all the earthquakes that Christchurch, NZ, endures almost daily. We enjoyed the Zoo in Sydney once again, as we had been to that Zoo with our Sons in 1986. So before departing Sydney, we called our Sons from a phone booth on the dock near the Sydney Opera House area. With such a technology jump, it was like calling next door.

From our initial departure in Fort Lauderdale, Florida on January 5, 2011, I had spent lots of free time on the stern deck. It was a perfect place for me to dig into Our Creator's Word and into "The Complete Guide to the Bible" by Stephen M. Miller. It was lite reading, but most informative about the "rest of the story" that the late Paul Harvey used to say. I had read the Bible cover to cover several times during my airline years, but needed a lite review to unclutter tons of thoughts. Mr. Miller's book did just that by lighting up the main points, using key words and verses to add biblical daily-life clarity, storyline flow and understanding.

Our stop in Cairns was a repeat for my Sweetheart and I. Our first time in Cairns was during our Airline Era, when we dove in the Great Barrier Reef and we saw huge clam like shells that could have swallowed most divers. From a previous trip to Palau, an island to the North of Cairns, we had experienced some beautiful beginner reef diving, where we just floated and let all the fish peak into our goggles and nibble on our arm hair's. In comparison, the magnitude of the Great Barrier reef was almost scary; especially after seeing those huge clam shells, and the thoughts of Great White Sharks. But what we still remember to this day about Cairns, from that previous trip while stationed in Guam, was our canoe trip through the nearby rain forest. Nevertheless, it was an awesome experience! I had overloaded myself with canoe steering and camera duties; then my Sweetheart looked up and saw a coiled black boa lying on a branch immediately above. Then I looked up. Since we both looked up at the same moment, guess what, our tipsy canoe tipped over and into the water we went. We lost some sun glasses along with getting soaked, and I am almost positive that I heard the boa laugh. Probably on the payroll.

Continuing our Holland America Cruise northerly, next stop was Papa New Guinea. This island stop was new to both our cruise company, and my Sweetheart and I. We were the first cruise ship to have docked at what had been an old German submarine port. The first thing that I noticed was that their crows were brown, but spoke the same "caw." Their bats were enormous and looked like eagles while flying. The locals were reserved and typically, like the indigenous people of Australia, spoke perfect Queen's English. So, shopping their market was most enjoyable and full of smiley entrepreneurs. Probably from my Norwegian heritage, I love anything made from wood; thus, we now have a very nice wood fruit bowl that has found a home in Florida.

And continuing northbound, we were supposed to revisit Palau as per our itinerary, but so popular, no place to anchor, or tie up to provide us with-to-be-expected first-class standards. Holland American is totally first class, so exit left and off to the Philippines. Around the Clark Air Force base and Manila area,

I have spent tons of both military time and airline time. And of course, entrenched with those forever memories of my jungle survival time among those jungle rats and snakes. From there, direct to Hong Kong. Been there numerous times and left with a memory of spectacular dancing harbor lights; similar to a northern aurora lights dance. my other memory, or thought, was why did my new Reeboks cost the same in Hong Kong as they do in Florida? I guess, no more good deals as China is emerging. So now onto Vietnam, we docked not too far from Bien Hoa, where I had been stationed in 1968-69. I thought about taking a cab, but did not want to risk another "tour," should I miss my boat departure for whatever reason.

Then onto Singapore, the cleanest city, best managed city in the world and exactly 180 earth degrees from Florida, or half way around the world from Florida. I was aware of the earthquake that had hit Christchurch, NZ, while we were northbound toward Hong Kong, and had impacted the church that we had just visited. And now another earthquake that hit the Sendai area of Japan; plus, a resulting and devastating tsunami on March 11, 2011. The cruise ship TV news showed the damaged jetway at the Sendai airport, the very same jetway that I pulled my airline B757 into several times. my airline flew to several Japanese airports out of Guam as well as Hong Kong, Vietnam, Philippines, Bali, Australia and numerous islands around the Pacific Ocean. Deep within, the Pacific Ring of Fire is constantly active with its on-going tectonic processes, or its large-scale shifting of plates. And with high probability, caused this area earthquake and ocean surface tsunami disaster near Sendai. The flight route from Guam to Sendai flew near an ongoing forming island with its noticeable flame cracking the surface; thus, outwardly pointed out how active our mother earth still is. This route was also near where President Bush Senior, a fellow fighter pilot, was rescued from the sea during WWII.

The Sendai news and pictures really hit home, and it only got worse! In Singapore, my Sweetheart and I were 12 hours ahead of Florida time and as 8:02PM rolled around for Mom and I, our Precious youngest Son, was instantly rescued by Jesus during an intersection accident, at 8:02AM Florida time, March 11, 2011. Mom and I were totally unaware until I stumbled upon an email to call home on a Sunday night, or two days later. His big Brother had the ugly, life changing role as the man-in-charge of this family situation.

I had that duty as well when my parents passed from old age, sad of course, but acceptable. However, losing a younger Brother was life-ripping for big Brother, but big Brother stepped up and did a marvelous handling of everything. And I mean everything, and as Dad, so glad that he did, because Mom and I felt like we were run over by a Mack truck. For me, I still tear up as if it just happened as I type this, but what gets Mom and I through every day, is our Faith in Our Creator Father and His Spiritual Energy ability to resurrect, to "Rapture" any-and-all accident victims, the unborn victims, and anyone or everyone who has never openly rejected Our Creator Fathers open arms.

I personally feel there is ample evidence to prove my case beyond the shadow of doubt. Although I did not pass the mankind bar exam, I think a jury of inner "small" voices will see or share the light and sense a new confidence once the "Donkey" takes the stand. I have obligated myself to Honor Our Creator Father as He honored my deepest need for His presence on a clear night in the Indian Ocean, while heading for India. Mom and I had stopped our formal dining and used mostly room service, as all I wanted to do was sit outside on the balcony, or walk the decks, cry and ask Father "WHY?"

After several nights on the balcony, with clear skies and lots of stars to stare at, from deep in my soul, I asked Father why did His Son Jesus ask: "Why has Thou Forsaken Me" and then I asked Father: "Where are You when I need You!" Boy did I hit the jackpot for the rest of my life!!! I will never forget How Our Creator Father Honored me and responded to my Faith that night. Father's Word states that He can and He has presented Himself several times. He presents Himself in ways that only the recipient will or would understand; thus, the coincidence rebuttal from others.

As I asked: where are You when I need You? Father answered instantly with a continuous fiery rope from high in the Heavens, aimed directly between my eyes and down into the "very" nearby horizon; noticeably close, almost as if it would hit the boat. I had never seen such a rope-like display from such a high altitude before, or could compare it to any past experiences. That visual stills lives fresh in my memory. Missiles and rockets only show lit plumes. Pilots know jerky, dancing flash lightning; plus, lightning originates much lower. I have been hit by lightning while flying; twice in the F-100, with the first time hitting on the nose. I lit up like a Christmas tree according to my wingman and knocked me back into my seat. Both lightning and/or static discharges do occur and can leave discharge evidence somewhere on the aircraft. Pilots also know the difference of falling stars, which mostly appear more shooting than falling, and always with the excitement knowing that the faraway stars and planets are alive and well.

Regardless, Our Creator's answer, and His visual response to my plea "is" forever entrenched in my mind. I continually look back to that moment. And my takeaway conclusion from such a firsthand, still crystal clear, visual observation, is that Our Creator is very real and definitely tied to the energy realm. Actually, it's much easier to explain Our Creator as Thee Awesome, Universe Mastermind, by using action terms connecting Our Creator to energy. More precisely, Our Creator is "Our Spiritual Energy Mastermind!!!" Thus, the remainder of my book will proceed with that thesis and reach.

Our Creator Daddy "was" listening back in Scene I, when I asked where did I lose my bag of pennies. I fully expect that He had been testing me, and most assuredly, nurturing me over the years, but now He was Honoring that Faith. He now had the right kid for the job to enlighten His world of His Spiritual use of "invisible" Energy and His direct connection to our "inner 'still small' voice." Plus, my youngest Son, probably put in a good word for his Dad. my resume started with farm boy awareness of animals such as the Donkey, awareness of gathered aviator wisdoms, awareness of our global earth, our galaxy and their universe relationships, and of course, awareness of His Word, cover-to-cover. But most of all, my aptitude-tested awareness of "electrical" properties or responses, and its around-the-clock "invisible" potential; yet, measurable as in a volt meter, or until one turns on a light switch. Yes, the juice is there, just "invisible," so never touch the medal on a electrical plug to avoid "shocking" consequences. Our Creator's Spiritual Energy connection to our "inner 'still small' voice," is acutely similar in concept. And by our body neural circuitry, connects our created invisible electrically natured responses to be uniquely recognized by Our Creator "Daddy" as "in His Own Image." Genesis 1:26-27. He loves and listens to Positive "Invisible Spirit Energies!!!" We can also touch His Word and we can expect to feel the emitting Positive Spirit Energies as well, just turn on your inner "small" voice and note how tranquil you feel. With His Word, I was "shocked" by its tangible, powerful life improving energies; yet invisible. More to follow!!!

Let's start with my lifetime accumulated perceptions and now in my opinion, a common sense understanding as to who Our Common Daddy really is and wants to be among or within His creation. No need for controlling religions or their monarchs, science monarchs, or political groups; just common-sense fun or happy stuff, like Our Daddy's wish to be Spiritually ever present among His kids, His Fatherly nature celebrated in kind and detailed through His legitimate Word, and so notarized by His use of the Cross as His signature on both His servant's back, or the Donkey's back; and most assuredly, the over 2000-year-old signature, His risen Son from His vacated Cross. Seems quite clear to me, my case should rest, but will let my reader jury decide. May I remind my readers that the similar crossed lines of an X was all that our legal arrangements required over the years as mutual acceptance. And so important to my overall storyline: that Our Creator Daddy seeks an "in His Image," a Positive Electrically Natured, Spiritual Relationship with His mankind creation, and guess what, another similar crossed lines of the "Plus" sign. Check any battery or electrical hardware worldwide. Yup, the accepted worldwide symbol for Positive electrical energy; so, is it a stretch that Our Creator Daddy chose the Cross during His Creation period as His personal signature sign, or symbol? Surely, Our Creator would know our future. Hence, the need to create an enduring servant to humbly carry His Notary Stamp. And may I add: This servant must outwardly reflect Our Creator Daddy's Nature and Personality to Serve His Creation!!!

‣ With RY

Since March 11, 2011, not a day goes by without some emotional tickle in my inner "small" voice; most likely from our youngest Son who has an immediate connection at His choosing. And as Mom and I broke out of our shell of grief during the ongoing, around the world cruise, we had much to be appreciative for. The Cruise Captain, his staff, our deck friends and our dining table partners had kept our cabin full of fragrant flowers. Our minds were more or less blasé as we sailed to ports in India, then from Mumbai onto Dubai, then onto Muscat, Oman. There we found Frankincense and Myrrh, or besides Gold, what the three wiseman brought as gifts during the Birth of Jesus. Now that was a "cool" find for me personally.

After Muscat, our cruise would now head for the Suez Canal, like the Panama Canal, another trip highlight wishes for my Sweetheart and I. But first a stop in Salalah, also in Oman. It's importance to me personally, was that it is said to be the home of Job from the oldest book in Our Creator's Word. Why is that important, because the Book of Job defines our Creator as to His kind and reliable Positive nature, and always full of Goodness, Grace and most of all, His Love!!! In short, a complete definition of a Redeeming Father. Job 19:25. Memories of Salalah will always be a visual, huge shipping distribution center like Fed Ex and UPS combined.

The Somali pirates were active, so departing for the Red Sea, I noticed our Navy covering our "six;" plus, our cruise Captain had prepped for the pirates with some sort of directional deafening sound device and water cannons. I had a superb view from deck six to offer some guard duty time; with a glass of wine as my weapon of choice. I had never noticed how long the Red Sea really is until this trip. I continually tried to determine which mountain off to our starboard, would be Mount Sinai.

We first turned starboard to Aqaba, Jordan and from there, took a bus trip up to Petra, known as the "lost city." What a nice experience. En route, we saw a few nomad tribes with their camels, and herds of sheep and goats; still residing in huge tents. And in Petra, I had my first Camel ride, which turned out be a three-phase process just getting on and up on all four legs. my takeaway memory was how terrible they treated their rather small Arabian horses. They must have been city kids; definitely not respectful horse lovers like me. While there and elsewhere on this cruise, I would check out any Donkeys that I saw. And yes, they all had natural Crosses on their backs.

When the Suez Canal opened in 1869, it thereafter changed the landscape of the area from during the time of Moses. I attempted to visualize all the obstacles that Moses and the Jewish nation had to deal with as they departed their Egyptian captors. Other than that, it was rather anticlimactic and now, just another waterway, yet pays huge dividends to world commerce.

I kept my eye on the Sinai area as we proceeded toward Israel. I could only imagine how challenging it must have been for Moses and his followers. That perception of the area started while in the Petra area.

Forty years of that, no wonder Our Creator had to step in and provide the daily edibles. No wonder the Jewish nation began to respect and honor their inner "spiritual" voice connection to Our Creator. Our cruise docked in Ashdod. almost straight west of Jerusalem, where tourists love to visit, but my Sweetheart and I wanted to go spend a day in the life of Sir Jesus. A local Islam driver did just that as we proceeded around a country about the size of our home county back in Florida. We headed for the Sea of Galilee, with visit stops at Megiddo, then Nazareth and then onto several stops around the Sea of Galilee itself. Starting with lunch at St Peters Restaurant, with a view of the Golan Heights to the east; we enjoyed some "must" dining of fresh fish from the Sea and next via Capernaum to the Church of Multiplication.

In all of Israel and for the rest of our lives, my Sweetheart and I will never forget this place. We sort of just drifted around the grounds and ended up going in different directions, but as we eventually drifted back together, we shared our uninfluenced, unusual internal perceptions of a very noticeable inner peace and its quelling comfort of our loss of our Youngest. Definitely more than an anecdotal experience, as it was totally bodily surreal and forever memorable; that Our Creator Father was comforting us and confirming that He was now caring for Precious Ry. Personally, I think Jesus keeps an earth residence there; did not see it, but sure felt it!!! As if I had been served a Valium cocktail!!! A Flight Surgeon gave me some Valium once after flying several hours straight in an F-4 and caused some back spasms, so I knew the feeling. So notably comforting at the time, that it was almost scary, but yet felt so welcome.

At this point in our world cruise, I was totally satisfied with the cruise in general; especially, with our stop in Israel. The overall peace that I felt among the people throughout our travels in Israel and outwardly noticed among the children as well, clearly revealed that my close stairwell friend, now Mr. Army General, had earned his stripes as the father of the trusted air defense security system.

Now onto a stop in Ephesus, Turkey to visit the last known home of Mother Mary, and an evening of dine and wine within a Roman built complex. A symphony under a full moon and stars, among pillars engraved with Roman words like Caesar, whoever he was, but on this night, April 9, 2011, my Grampa Lars' birthday, the Thompson's from Montana, North

Dakota and now nestled in Florida, were in town. Uber had not started its success story yet, but if they had, my Sweetheart and I would have taken a chariot back to the boat.

Several stops throughout the Mediterranean were in our itinerary, but I did look forward to docking in Spain. I and my Sweetheart seem to have a sweet spot and sweet memories for their culture. Back when I was flying B747's, my Sweetheart tagged along on a flight to Madrid. Spanish beer and olives won her over; plus, on the return trip to NYC, she got the entire first-class upstairs, the B747 upper deck all to herself. And on this cruise, we sure did enjoy cruising through the Straits of Gibraltar, with Europe on the right and Africa on the left; then a European wrap stop in Cadiz, Spain. Except for Dunedin, New Zealand, probably the most fun city to walk around on the cruise. Cadiz exuded so much personality cultured over time, and that in itself, suggested an area active with an ongoing "Happy Hour" history. Columbus also started from a nearby Port called Palos de la Frontera in 1492, then sailed toward America, or more precisely toward the East Indies. But all he had was God-Provided-Sense or the GPS of that era; so, he landed in our nearby Bahamas, probably

149

discovered local sailor's grog and possibly enabled American Happy Hour thinking with a Spanish flavor and flamenco dancing. Whatever he did, he still got his own holiday on our American calendar. He did get the Santa Maria sunk off the Haitian Coast; boy do I understand how easy that can be after a sailing trip through North Carolina and up to Maine. Even with Satellite GPS, it can be tricky when weather dictates your course.

Finally got to see the Madeira Islands, our last stop on this around the World Cruise, before our six-day return cruise to Fort Lauderdale. my Sweetheart and I were still in a daze over the loss of our Youngest and in all honesty, still am to this day. A loss of child is forever. I, at least, had the benefit of Our Creator's visual answer to my soul wrenching there in the Indian Ocean. At least, I know Our Creator Father is actively Real; that His Word and His Promises are present tense Real. That He surely has His Son Jesus by His side, and most of all, that He did honor His "Word," its promises, and that our Youngest was in His midst as well!!!

Our Youngest had been to Bible camp with his Pastor Uncle and cousins during his pre-adolescent years. In that setting, he had given his life to Jesus;

plus, recorded that moment in his Bible. Again, in all honesty, I needed those words of confirmation more than our Youngest did. He had such a beautiful soul and wore it on his sleeve like His Grandmother Evelyn. He was a natural zoo keeper from birth; his shadow, Cool Breeze, a Rottweiler-Chow mix, were inseparable. He handled and walked around animals with the Faith of Daniel. Something I wish I had the night I slept in that Philippine jungle. However, I need to openly give Our Creator Father, my recognition that He has always covered my six, the greatest Fighter Pilot's "Wingman" ever!!!

Upon our cruise arrival back in Florida, we said our adieus, but no farewells. After hanging out with fellow mariners for 110 days, birds of feather friendships evolve. So many of the passengers, treat the boat like a floating assisted living home and just continue from one cruise to the next. That would have been easy, but my Sweetheart Mom and I had a new life changing direction to resolve. We had acquired a large SUV and loaded 16 bags of luggage. We started with 18, as we were initially allowed to bring two cases of wine on board, which somebody drank. We headed across alligator ally to the western side of Florida, or the gulf coast with blank thoughts as to what we would find. We initially headed to the intersection accident location of our Youngest. At the time, it seemed vanilla, but over the years, I have visited it several times to analyze it like a Bar Exam question. All the money in the world could never bring my Youngest back, nor ever satisfy my internal whatever that keeps me tearing up at the drop of hat. So that was never the reason for my on-location analysis, but what was noticed was the propensity of left turn drivers, from their short-left turn lane, to challenge or crowd late yellows that suddenly changed to red. I personally perceive that situation may have led to my Youngest going westbound toward his home, two miles away, then hitting the tail end corner of a truck that may have just gone through a sudden-red left turn light.

All in a blink of eye; yet, totally irrelevant as accidents are accidents and I cannot reboot the situation. So glad that our Youngest had and lived a great life. Starting with skiing the Italian Alps at the age of three and a half between Dad's legs, skiing the California Cascades, skiing the Colorado Rockies and then returning to Lake Tahoe to fulfill a young man's dream of a winter job with a view; plus, ladies and learning the new art of snow-boarding.

While in his teens, he followed his big brother and his parents around British Columbia and several Pacific countries, to include Bali as well; thus, he had enjoyed a large chunk of Our Creator's earth world. So how do we deal with accidents; better yet, how does Our Creator handle split second or instant situations? That is largely the challenge for this book; plus, the desire to answer my Matthew 28 commission to spread the Gospel. From that intersection, we proceeded to our Youngest home, where we saw a miraculous, totally obvious effort by our oldest Son and his fellow law partners to ease the pain for "we" the parents. Then highlighted by an alter arrangement to display our Youngest's Bible, opened to where he had accepted Jesus. I am not big on coincidences, but our Youngest was taken at 34, noticeably close to the same age that Jesus was resurrected. I can live with the happy thought that they are on the same team these days to serve Our Creator Father. Therefore, I do just that and write on, knowing that I am Blessed!!! Most of my tears these days, are those of Gratefulness for Our Creator's "Blessed Assurances!!!"

➤ my Lifetime of Observations, Thinking; and of course, my Opinions

Our Creator's vivid reply answer there in the Indian Ocean, was forever mentally indelible and so timely. For years, I would question Him about Faith, how much Faith, answer me please!!! Well He did, never to be forgotten, nor questioned again. Even our Youngest has let Mom and Dad know that all is well, or as he used to say, "it's all good Dad." One morning, back a few years, I was doing my routine glances at a happy moment picture with our Youngest wearing his G'day sweatshirt that we bought during our family visit to Australia in 1986. Probably not surprising, we keep several fond memory pictures strategically located around the house.

While standing there looking at his picture, my new iPhone down in my Bermuda shorts side pocket, started making odd sounds. So I took it out only to hear not music, but strangely familiar words. I had recently learned about Pandora and had added the App. I normally only listen to country, dinner time piano, Native American flute and Hymns on Sunday, but all I heard was a voice, no singing or music. This was totally unexpected to me as I thought Pandora only dealt in music.

This voice proceeded to talk about the Tsunami in Japan on March 11, 2011—so Mom and I listened most intently that morning. It talked about a phone booth that survived and was left standing, and that all the family grieving survivors would come there, and use this empty, "not" hooked up phone booth to call their lost family members. Mom and I had called our Youngest from a similar phone booth in Sydney, Australia. Totally far out, but our Youngest had found a way to call home symbolically; plus, tie it to his March 11, 2011 accident, and tell Mom and Dad that all is well, or "it's all good Dad!!!"

I later found out that something called a podcast can also be included on Pandora. I would never have added or picked a talking podcast station as one of my Pandora stations. I am only into Pandora primarily for the country music and for soft dinner piano music. But what are the odds on that particular podcast would start up while in my pocket; especially, since I had never heard of it beforehand, nor knew that it even existed. When I finally located it, I found it among over 600 podcasts to choose from. For those who would like to hear this podcast: not sure of the recording company but on Pandora, it's number 597. The title does not reach out and tell you it's about the March 11, 2011 Japan Tsunami, as it's titled "one last thing before......" Anyway, both Mom and I see this as our Youngest reaching out from his spiritual balcony and using the phone booth symbolically to reverse call and comfort his Mom and Dad that he is OK! He was always proud of his private pilot license, and as Dad, I was equally proud of him. Probably silly, but I can take rest, knowing that he is now a Universe Pilot. And I can take rest by living in Faith and Spiritual Concert with Our Creator Father, as guaranteed by the Cross, and become a Universe Pilot someday as well.

⯈ Opinion Number One: The Pathway back to Our Creator and His Blessed Assurance

So, the title of this book is Honoring Our Creator and my tagline is by Honoring Our Inner "small" Voice. Now after my short bio, the big question that now needs more polish is how do we interact where personal doubt is no longer, over forever, done, period, Amen!!! For me, it only took two words to lock in my "Blessed Assurance" confidence forever. my career affiliation with these two words made it easy. They became integral to my life early on and these two words are: ENERGY AND POSITIVE.

The word Energy was definitely on display in Our Creator's creation period as written in His Word or in Genesis. Problem was, it was not a word yet, at least not a word familiar to all Our Creator's inspired scribes. Around 350BC, Aristotle probably coined the word, but not in time for the canonizing and press time of Our Creator's Word. Energy was surely the Means and the How behind Our Creator's "In His Beginning!!!" Energy is an all-purpose, universal power word to generalize how things become real, can be or will be; or, "How" things simply get done!!! And in Our Creator's Words, all things Visible or Invisible, and all things Tangible or Intangible got done!!! And Our Brilliant, so Cool Creator made all Energy interchangeable and never lost. How "cool" is that!!!

As I eluded in Scene II, my fighter pilot era, the word "Energy" was key to understanding the road to all successful missions, whether it be in terms of fuel, use of airspeed, altitudes, or any of the four forces for flight. But the daily mindset universal word around fighter squadrons, was how we would or should use our "Energy!" Even when my two Super Sons were growing up, I would seek their "Love Energy Hugs." Don't laugh, it truly worked for me. That all-encompassing word is entrenched into my DNA and my redefining and refining Our Creator, and His means to run His Universe. And now as I dig into the Laws of Energy, I am intrigued by the fact that Energy is never lost, can be changed or altered, but never lost. Fighter pilots attempt to employ that same concept and used an "energy preserving, vertical egg" during air-to-air combat flying, in order to preserve our best aircraft designed corner velocities for whenever needed. Our created energy within our Universe or beyond, is Our Creator's "means" to do His thing as Our Common "Daddy," or with His Spiritual Arms and Hands.

When I joined the Air Force, they gave me an aptitude test, well I almost flunked mechanics, but got a perfect score in electronics. So off to school up in Illinois, and memories of those cold wet winds coming south from Lake Michigan. That turned out be another Blessing. Later on, I was able to rewire my 27 O'Day sail boat for all the comforts of home. Drew out the circuitry on a piece of scratch paper and everything is still working after sailing from Florida to Maine.

To understand anything or its associated concepts, it's always best to learn it in its most simple understanding. When I started my law school studies while stationed in Europe, the program started with the beginnings of king made law, later judge made law, then the writings of Oliver Wendell Holmes on common law. The most basic approach to understanding law itself, was through a mindset of who's hands are clean and who's hands are dirty. Statue law is as written, and like our Constitution, is more-cut-and-dry; thus, easier to understand and apply. And if all hands are clean, then it's Happy Hour negotiations, or bar-court rounds settled with rock, paper, scissors. My six-year-old Granddaughter taught me that, and if life conflicts were only that simple and fun.

In electronics, a simple running water learning concept works well. Just think of visible, tangible wet water in lieu of invisible, intangible charged particles flowing through a pipe or wire, and its either on through the faucet or switch, or off. The world of electricity can be measured in potential, yet invisible; thus, suggesting an "energy" standing by to serve. Does that sound like anybody we know and have been Honoring? Sort of sounds like a "parent" figurehead.

Continuing with "simple," consider our world of electricity as if it was all stored in a huge car battery and lets "simply" call it a huge Universe battery. Why a car battery, well it has a Positive aspect, or pole and a negative aspect or pole. Both are essential for it to work as a useable "energy" form; otherwise, it's mute like lots of planets. A car battery is designed to hold potential "energy" to start the car upon request and even a little occasional prayer request when its old and cold outside. I remember a lot of that growing up in NW North Dakota. Conceptually, in "my Opinion," can translate an understanding "How" Our Creator does His thing, should we need His "potential," or Him instantly. A car battery usually comes with a switch device; such as a car key to turn on the "energy", so what turns on Our Creator Daddy to interact with our needs and prayers?

Our Creator is definitely in charge of all the Energy within our known Universe, and of course, beyond what we know as well. But what turns on Our Creator Daddy, well Jesus said that Our "Daddy is a Spirit." John 4:24. And like any Dad, in "my Opinion," is simply swooned by "Positive Spiritual Responses" from His family, as we were created "in His image," and to be heard via our inner "small" voices. Our words of Prayer that excite Faith, Hope, Trust, Expect, and most of all Love, surely exude Positive Spiritual Energy "Worship and Truth," through our inner "small" voice; which also completes John 4:24.

Recall that He gave us the power of "choice" during our creation. Why? So again, in "my Opinion," that we might know the difference between Positives and negatives; or more spiritually related, as in Positive Love and/or negatives. The power of choice suggests that perfection maybe the desired aspiration, but is "not" required. The only perfect people noted in Our Creator's Word, that I would presume perfect were Elijah, Enoch, John the Baptist, his Father Zechariah, His Mother Elizabeth, and of course Mother Mary and her famous One-of-Kind Son, JESUS. Other than these, imperfection is evidenced throughout Our Creator's Word as several of His major players had life blemishes and were still chosen for their obvious Positive qualities. It becomes obvious that Our Creator Father is a Positive Spiritual Entity and matches up well with Positive Faith mindsets here on His Earth. Like a true Father, forgives negatives in a flash and rewards Positives. Most notable in the New Testament, Saul Paul, as I call him. Our Creator called on Mister "previously negative Saul" to write most of the Positive New Testament as a repentant Positive Paul; after His Son, JESUS returned to His rightful position next to His Creator Daddy.

Rather obvious in Our Creator's Word; especially, the Gospels and with JESUS clarifying the difference between the Old Testament Laws with their "overtones of fear" and the New Testament parental-style covenant of "Goodness, Grace and Love." Then abide and live One simple daily Commandment: "Love thy Creator Father and Love thy Neighbor." Thus, generating an internalized Positive Spiritual Energy for everyone to enjoy and reciprocate; especially, "to" Our Creator Father. I and Positive Believers expect that Our Creator can and will answer prayer and even do miracles within the Positive realm of Spiritual Energy. Judging from His history, personal Faith Energy always benefits and rewards those who seek him. Not sure how Our Creator interacts with the negative aspects of the Energy realm, but I fully suspect that rejections to, or via one's inner "small" voice, leaves Our Positive Energy Creator helpless; until you change and communicate via your inner "Spirit" voice, with enough Positive Faith Energy to boost your "body electrical energy" signature to the size of a "mustard seed." Matthew 17:20. Lite

"Siri" research connects our "inner voice" to our nervous system, or referred to as our "electrical information highway." Sounds like Energy Circuit talk to me; thus, in "my Opinion," Our Creator's "Spiritual Energy" becomes connected via "In His Image" to our individual "Spiritual Energy" Circuit, or to our inner voice circuit. Obviously, this was by design, so why not just keep it simple: Believe in Our "Obvious" Creator Daddy and live in a Jesus-Style-Simple-Daily-Faith. Then Honor Our Creator by expecting to be Raptured into Our Father's Spiritual Heaven like the Gospel's Parodical Son, if and when needed, or rescued during a car accident such as my youngest Son required. But be careful and leery of life traps, such as creeping man-led political and/or religion hypocrisies. Now near 80, I have zero fear of passing, and I hope and wish that I pass-on with a smile on my face as a grateful tribute to my Creator "Daddy," for all my Life Blessings.

I do know that negatives, are a necessary part to understanding electronics, as without it, nothing works, even lightning. Negatives are mute until the existences of attracting Positives in their midst, and that sums up, in my opinion, our Universe. Lite "Siri" research, revealed that the earth as well as

163

most planets, are largely inert and were apparently created and/or designed by Our Creator as negative receptors. The stars, or our Sun was created with infusion capabilities in order to produce light, and in Genesis, lit up most likely by a Positive energy "spark" from Our Creator.

So back to the other key word, "choice," to understand Our Creator Daddy's binary workings in our Universe, and most of all, an understanding how Our Creator Daddy needed to work with us. Our Daddy gave His mankind creation, or each of us "individual choice." Why? So simply think of anyone that has not had to think or survive for themselves. Our Creator knew full well that his kids had to think for themselves in order to survive, and like a true leader, accepted the risk that mankind might not discover Him, nor answer or listen to their inner "small" voices while trying to survive. Thus, the dilemma that Our Creator Daddy faced for hundreds, or even thousands of years after His Creation of mankind. Then out of an arid area on His planet, an enslaved, signaling Jewish Nation became large, dependent and pleadingly needy; thus, Our Creator Daddy finally had a candidate group reaching for guidance. Therefore, and thereafter, Our Creator was able to get in concert Spiritually with mankind via the Jewish Nation, and summarily delivered to All mankind, His Fatherly Goodness and Grace; plus, wrote His "Word."

The choice ability given to mankind is in concert with the Universe binary use of Positives and negatives to facilitate the "How" Our Creator Daddy can respond to our spiritual prayers and requests. Again in "my Opinion," Energy and its many transmutable forms are the "Means" and gives Our Creator that omnipotent or unlimited capability and power to say in Genesis that "all things are possible through Our Creator Father." And now quickly back to my "in the beginning," I recall similar words from Bible school, or from someone back then. Thus, my personal positive belief, my mindset, or whatever generated that attitude back then, did me well over the years. I have been superbly Blessed because, in my Opinion, I probably gave my Spiritual Daddy enough Positive belief, at least the size of a "mustard seed," the day when I asked him where my "bag" of pennies was. With that, my and/or Our Creator Daddy stuck with "Positive-thinking" me through thick and thin, and provided me the how and the means along the way to enjoy a Super Blessed life!!! Within these book

165

pages, I have the opportunity to tell everyone that my or Our Creator Daddy has been sending me "pennies" from His chest of Blessings all along, and with my name on them. Since my Faith was in His pocket from my youth, I just had to seek, ask, trust and as Joel Osteen adds, think bold and expect! And I think that Joel's greatest daily advice to all his admirers is to simply "live in agreement" with Our Creator Daddy. And of course, add Dr. Gail Brenner's words of advice, "get out of our own way" and let Our Creator Daddy do His thing!!! Amen!!! Joel definitely deserves my accolades in his endeavors to Honor Our Creator. Plus, after I finish this book, I will seek the movie "pennies from Heaven," to see if there is a similar respectful appreciation of Our Creator. This book is meant to go public, so publicly, I Thank You, my Creator Father!!!

Recall that I stated above that Our Creator needs to work by Himself in His Universe as Positive-likes repel and might cause a mass universe explosion, probably worse than the "Black Hole." Or, that "collapsed star" situation as maybe the result of a "repel situation," or responses to similar electromagnetic interrelationships that continue within our Universe. Nevertheless, by Himself, all things are possible.

Individual personal Positives such as Hope, Faith and the Greatest is Love, 1 Corinthians 13:13, have powerful Spiritual Energy qualities. Every living person knows the power of Love and so does Our Creator, who designed that triggered sensation into our personal DNA. Even animals can sense Love and return their affection! When revealed to Our Creator Daddy, He can use the inspired "Spiritual Energy" to enrich our lives, or to save us, should an instant need arise. Outward Positive actions, or Positive words that are emitted spiritually via our inner "small" voice are unlimited. However, Our Creator Daddy gave us a heads-up in His Word that He thinks like any Father or parent would; that the best word is "Love!!!" But feelings and words like Faith, Trust, and even the word Expect, are just a few that transmit Positive immediate responses as in Spiritual Hugs to Our Creator Daddy. Personally, I think that the word "Expect," really Honors Our Creator and His Genesis Mantra that nothing is impossible for Our Creator. Amen!!! And no, Our Creator Father does not take an Expect attitude as spoiled, but rather Honors His "I AM, WHO I AM!!!"

However, it only takes "one" negative word of rejection to negate Our Creator Father's ability to give you everlasting, eternal spiritual life. The fear teaching mongers of my youth loved to scare you, in hopes of keeping one from going to "hell," or a place with negative consequences. That approach seemed like an insult to Our Creator Daddy, who stands behind the Parable of the Parodical Son and reveals His Fatherly Love. Our Creator Daddy owns the Universe and deals in Positive choices, certainly not fear, and will surely detect any Positive energy anywhere and everywhere. But if he cannot sense any Positive energy, it's like turning off an electrical switch and Our Creator Daddy will sense zero energy, or sadly, a rejection. And therefore, "hell" in "my Opinion," is explained in "short" for getting left behind and summarily, an eternal "dirt nap." Unless, of course, that Revelations 22:12-16 might override my lay understanding, as nothing is Impossible for Our Creator Daddy. So, where is "hell?" In "my Opinion," we are walking on it.

However, back in 2017, I did encounter a hell of sorts, like any hell or any uncomfortable situation, it takes lots of preplanning, a keyword to avoid any undesirable, negative consequences. This one is listed in the sailors' bible, called the Eldridge Tide and Pilot Book. And it's called Hell Gate. Sailing from Florida to Maine, one would eventually arrive in the magnificent NYC. After aviating for 14 years out of the nearby Newark airport, entering the New York City harbor by sail, was quite an experience and almost as busy on the water, as it is downtown. Sailing past the Statue of Liberty and taking a selfie was quite an unique experience, while dodging numerous ferry and tourist boats. I leased a slip for thirty days in Jersey City and conveniently next to a PATH or subway station. A perfect place to share an open boat bunk, so my brother-in-law, a retired Pastor, from Montana, joined me for some fun times from Central Park north to Wall Street south. Plus, my Super Son flew up just to escort his Dad and his Pastor Uncle to a Yankee game up in the Bronx via a somewhat new service called Uber, an unforgettable, uniquely New York memory.

Pastor and I tried to get in cycle with the crowds that attended the outdoor NBC morning show, but we were always late; even at 3-4am. Over the years, I have learned that any show at Radio City Music Hall is always enjoyable, or any show on Broadway as well; thus, scripting my life within this book, in scenes, seemed so applicable. All during this time, I was preplanning how to depart the NYC harbor safely via a challenging waterway referred to as "Hell Gate" and into the Long Island Sound. Yup, spelled H-E-double L. Studying the sailor's bible on tides and Hell Gate itself, reminded me of studying Our Creator's Bible to find His Blessings and to avoid the negatives. To avoid any consequences of a hellish situation; such as the biblical "hell" that is implanted within our minds from our youth, one should seek the recorded learned wisdoms from the past and others. Thus, I studied the word so to speak, and I sought counsel with anyone and everyone who had ever sailed through Hell Gate. The primary reason why I needed to take it very serious, was that the currents could easily overpower my ten horse power diesel engine and my normal speeds of 5-6 knots. The answer was seemingly simple, but like a shuttle launch, it had to be timed perfect. So, a month later, we launched from the Hudson River side and nailed the timing perfectly during flood tide flowing northeast; then witnessed GPS speeds more than twice my normal sailing speeds as we whistled through unforgiving rocky narrows and onward up the Long Island Sound.

What am I saying? To avoid any confusing inner voice messaging, or any hellish-like potential or situation, seek applicable wisdoms, or more importantly, seek Our Creator's Word; such as the Gospels. Hang your hat on every word, enjoy it word-for-word, as the answers and rewards are out-of-this-world!!! Get the picture??? In the Gospels, one will discover that Sir Jesus, took care of all perceived "Hell Gate" issues upon the "Cross." John 19:30. We, His people, just need to recognize the Gospel's wisdoms or the slack currents; such as, the Faith the size of a "mustard seed," Matthew 17:20, and/ or the safe waters offered to us during our lives on mother earth. Then respectfully Honor His gift of eternal, everlasting life. John 3;16. And in "my Opinion, since every reader should be tuned in by now, Honor His Donkey sidekick as well, as Our Creator Daddy's' preplanned Blessed "Insurance" of "Blessed Assurance!!!"

So, I must repeat what I stated above and always keep this in mind, it also only takes "one" Positive energy word to give you eternal life, even if you change your mind in the last split second. This luxury is promised by His Word that the sincere last can be first or before the self-judging hypocrites, Matthew 20:15-16, and with just the Positive "Belief" of a "mustard seed!!!" And No "works" required!!!

Ephesians 2:8-10. These verses of Our Creator's Promises are a true "Godsend" for all who serve in their country's military, or the conflicted and wavering.

Jesus gave us a prayer format in His Gospels and told us to first honor Our Creator Father, then within the prayer, by asking Him to forgive our trespasses. The word trespasses implies' "passing through" and in "my Opinion," suggests the passing through from good to wrong; then back to good. Or, to my way of thinking in terms of energy, from Positive to negative; back to Positive. Thus, Our Creator Father is able to respond with Blessings, or if needed to rescue Positive believers and bring them to His Eternal Home.

Jesus also informed us in His Gospels of Our Creator Father's "Unpardonable Sin", and if understood within the realm of energy logic, it translates to a "lost opportunity." However, in Our Creator Father's Universe and with mankind created "In His Image," recall that we were given choice during our creation. Thus, any change of heart, like a true Father, He forgives faster than a flash of lightning. No fear; just Love!!! Any spark of Positive Belief like Faith, Hope, Trust, and Love, in the size of a mustard seed, provides enough Positive energy to propel anyone back to Our Creator Father's realm of Goodness and Grace. Amen!!! And by the way, "NO" works are necessary, so no excuses.!!! And by the way, recall that Our Creator Daddy's Word has been notarized, by His Humble Servant, the Donkey!!! And Yes, the trail of Donkey continues!!!

No one would expect me to say that I have had a Blessed life after losing my youngest Son, but accidents are just that, still accidents. That gut-wrenching aftermath came close to sending me into negative territory. But fortunately, I learned to trust Our Creator prior and I have witnessed His hand full of Positives; thus, I turned everything over to him in that situation. I sense my youngest Son is fine, always near and now we can be a team with His great connections to "Honor Our Creator." So, in 2015, I took a leap into the unknown; with a Matthew 28 "commission" mission mindset and with a worldwide social media called Twitter as my outreach missionary.

⇥ creators2015voice.com

my 2015 worldwide Internet website endeavor: my website intentions were and still are, to Honor

Our Creator and His Son Jesus, by honoring "my" commission as stated in Matthew 28. In 2014, one of my close friends joined me for some sailing time from Florida and up to Savannah, Georgia. He brought his coffee cup, and on it said Matt 28. That cup left an itch in my soul and although I have read Our Creator's Word several times, I had glossed over the word "commission" over the years. While still in my aviating years, I had mentally assigned that task to actual missionaries. Well, to this highly Blessed veteran, it now sounded like an order. This close friend and I are essentially twins, except he was born 4 months and 4 days late. However, he beat me into the previously mentioned super-exciting Wild Weasel flying. So, we shared that and T-38 excitements in our Air Force years; plus, during our airline years, the B-747. Our Sweethearts are close friends as well and kept our family-like friendship directed to Our Creator and His influencing of our minds and deeds.

For years and after supporting missionaries and some that were family members as well, I thought that I might try a new approach. The Internet covered the globe by 2015, so why not use it and also use Twitter to be my outreach missionary. The use of magical "hashtags," like #WhosyourDaddy, empowers

Twitter to share common interest topics around the globe, across all races and/or religious lines. Plus, the capability of using key words to trigger search engines, like Google to reach the curious of all races, all faiths or all religions around the world. I found the perfect means, or worldwide vehicle to host my quest; rather poetic that Our Creator's "Word" could reach all His earth family via "Word" Press. So, Hello World!!! Word Press does all the heavy lifting, and also supports missionary-like outreach through social media. Sir Jesus stated desire was for all who had heard His gospels, was to pass it on "one to another." The word church, meaning then, the people; thus, pass His message on to people, via one to another. Eventually and today, the word church more or less, became thought of more as a physical building where "thee" people gather.

So, within the word press or WP network, I envisioned a cyber-church, meaning all of Our Creator Father's kids around the world. And like any leader greeting of an outreach forum, the website itself starts with "HELLO WORLD." Thus, my first posted blog on August 10, 2015, also started with: Hello World, my first name is Link. my first wish is that this website forum reaches every corner of every continent. All the social media aids will be used to hear from all individuals on Our Creator's Earth. Thus, my first question to kick off an ongoing Blog is: Who is Our Common Daddy, or Our Creator? Respectively, mankind is Blessed to have such an Awesome "Daddy" Deity!!! And my Spiritual pathway to fully comprehend Our Creator can be found in my About post. Respectively forget the opinions and teachings of religions and their leaders for now. Has Our Creator ever jiggled your Spiritual Soul from time to time? Did you let your Spiritual Soul respond, or just follow others, mores, or your senses? There are no right or wrong answers. Our Creator gave us the Power of Choice, which has the implicit learning curve, or commonly called Grace!!! my only caveat and learned recommendation, is to correlate your influences with your innate awareness of a Supreme Being, or Our Creator. Please know that this is a fully open forum, so Lets' Rock And Enjoy Knowing Our Creator Together!!!

During these times, I was mostly watching for reply comments and/or signs of followers, but it was mostly "Hmmm," must be doing something wrong, or too controversial. So I posted my second Blog on May 17, 2017: After starting my web-blog about our

Common Daddy, Our Creator, I decided to let my website cook and stew for a while and to monitor the amazing power of search engine key words and social media; such as Twitter and the use of hashtags. But it became time to stir the world pot with a summary post, then re-tweak this site and also retweet to find worldwide Twitter followers.

> Previous tweet: #whosourdaddy? Fishing in the dark to bring the light of the world back on #OurCreator, #OurCommonDaddy on web-blog: creators2015voice,wordpress.com

> Previous tweet: #WhosOurDaddy? Share your inherited heart and soul, Spiritual views from #OurCreator on web-blog: creators2015voice.com or @ creatorslink

> #whosourdaddy? Let's go around the world and Honor #OurCreator by sharing awareness of a Supreme Being on web-blog: creators2015voice.com

Still not the talk of the world or the town, but giving up is not in my DNA!!! Thus, prior to setting sails in May 2019, another posted blog entitled: Embrace the Challenge!!! In 2015, I began my desire to become Our Creator's Voice; not to be connected to religion, nor conflicted by religion. As a retired US Air Force Fighter Pilot with too many combat missions and with too much daily news of world conflicts, year after year, it was all ahead, full speed!!! Surely, it must "jokingly" be caused by a mankind "family feud," as we all have the same Creator Father. To Our Creator, this is never a joke; so, shame on all His Children.

Anyway, I decided to let my new Word Press website, started in 2015 and my initial blogs; plus, some teaser tweets to brew and stew. Now in my seventies, I needed to catch up with my understanding of Word Press, search engine concepts, hashtags, and of course, social media. During that time, I found two made-to-order books, "How to Blog a Book" and "Blogging for Writers." These two books are fantastic, kudos to the authors! These two books are like a pilot aircraft checklist.

In my website "About," I wrote that I would eventually compose a book, and since found these two great aids toward blogging a book; so, no more excuses. It's time to be "Honoring Our Creator," my chosen book title, and the expert book writers say to add a tagline; so, I have chosen to be "Honoring Our Inner 'small' Voice" as my tagline.

my wish is to share my "people watching" observations from travelling nearly the entire world; both as an Air Force Fighter Pilot and later as an International Airline Pilot. Additionally, my Sweetheart and I circled the world on our 40th Anniversary Cruise. From this starting Blog to a Book, I will expand on my people observations, and to impress no one, but only to HONOR OUR CREATOR and share.

my very next Blog, posted on May 22, 2019, is essentially Scene I or my "in the beginning" in this book. This year, 2020, I will celebrate my 79th Birthday and almost ready to have this book ready for the publishers. It is meant to reveal the growth of my awareness, devotion and understanding of Our Amazing Creator Daddy within the storyline of my so very Blessed life. So much more important is to reveal Our Creator Daddy's natural love and loyalty to His all Kids!!! And why the book of Job is the oldest book in Our Creator Father's WORD and so vital to our understanding of Our Creator as a "Daddy!!!"

And of course, the trail of the Donkey!!! Behold the GREAT AUTHENTICATOR, THE DONKEY AND ITS CROSS AND JESUS, AND HIS CROSS!!!

▸▸ The Armageddon Kids

As I was implementing my outreach endeavors, so was ISIS recruiting participants for evil endeavors by a twisted understanding of a man-made religion. my thinking was that I could replicate their Internet methods and means with "good" news about Our Common Daddy, Our Creator Father. But like TV programs about evil doers, evil news travels faster and seems to trump good news. Nevertheless, I embraced the challenge and went "fishing in the dark." I pressed on with teaser blogs to attract or excite responses. Lots of viewers, but no responses. Maybe the viewers were just CIA, DIA, FBI, OR NSA. If they looked closer, they probably would have noticed that I had been a T-38 Flight Instructor/Class Commander for such notables as the son of King Daoud of Afghanistan, Iranians under the Shah and Jordanians. All good kids back then, and except for transparent Jordan, their countries are since ruined by leaders of their religions.

As I write this book through blogging my thesis and main points, my website is still struggling, but I have no intention of quitting a pleasing, satisfying endeavor. In fact, when I noted China's President Xi was on Twitter, I tweeted an invite to become "pen pals." Thought I might soften President Xi, to permit my worldwide outreach into China. However, I think he is just on Twitter just to follow Trump. In my opinion and having been to China, I know just enough about Buddhism to know that they are about a half step away from becoming super Christians. They honor their inner "divine" self by becoming a "lamp unto your own feet." In so doing, their mantra became over time, that they can go through life alone without a higher deity, or at least that is how I understand their thinking. Much of the world population seem to live their daily lives that way, but probably do not enjoy the nirvana daily life that I sensed in my Far East travels through Buddhist areas. Hopefully, I did not mistake that impression for an actual suppression from dictator governments and a contained, penned-up demeanor.

Therefore, in "my Opinion," if the entire Buddhist religion concluded that their "In their Beginning" interpretation and our Universe "In the Beginning," was provided to them by non-other-than Our Common Daddy; then changed their thinking of their inner "divine self" to the "inner 'small' voice," that is tied to Our Universe Creator Father, we would have a serious jump in church attendance. my outreach to President Xi is a worthy start: bottom line is that I found all the people in the Far East from Indonesia north to Japan totally enjoyable and kind. They all have paid the price of man-made conflicts over politics, or in the name of man-made religions.

SCENE

V

my Wrap Epilogue

Nothing like a foot of fresh snow to tell you what a seventy-eight-year-old body and legs feels like after a few runs. But I did manage to accomplish my wish to ride the lifts and attack the Colorado slopes one more time; just to enjoy another run with my Wonderful Son, who started between my legs. my other desire was to surprise my Super Cool Grandchildren by falling within their midst and fill their memories of their crazy Grampa showing up on the slopes unexpected. It was the winter of 2019 and the whole northwest was blanketed with snow, even got stranded in Dillion, Colorado, by Interstate 70 avalanches. Apparently, that happens a lot in Dillion as they were sure ready with a local version of a Happy Hour at the Dam Brewery. Since I was in the "area," my brother-in-law and I revisited all our common nieces and nephews, that now include their families as well. Super memories continued as I think of all of them and their families as Uncle-Blessings, we dined and I was honored to pay as a Blessed Uncle should.

I know that my readers probably noted reiterations and/or repetitions, but from my aviation era, it's a habit that is hard to break. It's always vital that everyone who is a part of a flying mission, totally understand their role, so I have a habit of repetition and, or reiteration. To me, living in concert with Our Creator Daddy is totally vital, and that my perceived Spiritual Pathway picture back to Our Daddy becomes crystal clear; thus, the reiterations, Now some ending story basics: world conflicts seem so easy to stop and world peace seems so easy to achieve, provided that we think and honor each other as a family member of Our Common Daddy's Creation. I cannot emphasize enough that we all bleed red and have interchangeable parts. But, as I write this segment, religion politics are still in the way, and now, a coronavirus is in fact covering almost the entire earth population and everyone is vulnerable. Clearly pointing out that we all need each other, and that we all need to act like a unified family and cure this as a family. Religions that generate political puppets need to stop their divisive rhetoric and do something constructive like pursue the power of prayer for one another. After losing my bag of pennies as a child, I was skeptical; but since, I have witnessed that prayer works wonders.

As I eluded earlier or above, Our Creator did not create religions, and need not be a religion. His Son Jesus did not attend any seminaries; yet knew His Creator Father's Positive Natured Thesis and Wishes like the back of His hand. All of Our Creator's world-wide Family would be better served with a mindset of Positives versus negatives. As stated above, I have witnessed that prayer works and what is prayer, but an internalized Positive Spirit that is activated through our inner "small" voice; then, expressed outwardly with Positive attitudes, spoken words and deed. Our Creator can and will react to Positive expression with Positive Energy responses, leading to desired Positive outcomes. I witnessed such Positives first hand, there in the Indian Ocean in March 2011. And in all the feedback that I get from such children's hospitals as St Jude's and the Shriners; as well as from my niece's daughter, now in high school after a touch and go birth issue.

Personally, I see Our Creator everyday as I enjoy breakfast watching the Sun come up, watching the dolphins or fish jump, watching the manatees swim by and most of all, listening to Our Creator's bird choir sing. and then every time I get to babysit the Grandkids, or now days, when they babysit me. I see my Sons and Grandchildren as visual gifts from an Awesome Creator Father, via their also awesome Moms, whom Our Creator chose to be His Multipliers, Genesis 1:28. Then around 2000 years ago, Our Creator chose Mother Mary to be His Son's Mom, Luke 1:29-32. So, Moms' are Special, like Mom Evelyn and also Honored in my storyline.

The overwhelming consensus of our Astronauts was that there are no atheists in outer space. Even Einstein, a declared agnostic, confusingly declared that he was not an atheist; but simply concluded that all that is visible or invisible, and all that is tangible or invisible, must have had an "In the Beginning." So, it gives me great pleasure to exhibit current day evidence that Our Creator Father laid the trail of transparent authentication during and through His prophecies to inform mankind of His plan to come visit His creation in "Person." Our Father's authentication plan was, or is in plain sight for all to see, but so totally subtle, that it became over time, a common practice "innocent coverup," or sort of just covered up by blankets or riding cushions. Maybe innocent humor in this case, but nevertheless, an unnoticed "fact" on the back of a Donkey, a humble animal servant that would be used by Our Creator in His Word. The Donkey was in fact created well before the Birth of Jesus. The Donkey was created with a natural CROSS ON ITS BACK, ANOTHER FACT. The Donkey was always included in the prophecies regarding the coming of the Messiah, or the visit of Our Creator, as His Son JESUS. my lame joke of a coverup was that the Donkey's back was typically covered when serving whomever and went unnoticed; thus, the Donkey became just another servant animal and taken for granted. Therefore, not associated with any realm of greatness until this farm boy picked up on this significance during a grade school Christmas play. This play included my child nephew and also included a live Donkey. The class teacher casually mentioned the Cross on the Donkey's back as if a coincidence, but life has taught me that coincidences are actually the "Hand of Our Creator" in verifiable action. I had been a part of such Christmas plays during my grade school years as well, but never did we include live animals on stage. During my airline era and while aviating out of NYC, my family and I attended the Radio City Music Theatre, Christmas Spectacular numerous times. Their program included the Rockettes, but never noticed then when their Donkeys came on stage. Must have been all those Rockette's legs!

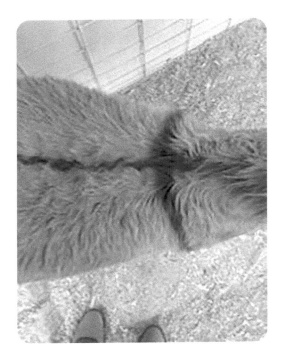

Thus, from that moment on, I have checked out every Donkey that I have seen since, and sure enough, they all have Crosses on their backs. From such plain view evidence on the Donkey's back, and surely after the crucifixion of Our Lord Jesus, upon a Cross, my simple deduction is that Our Creator Father planned to use the Cross as His Signature and to visit His Creation during HIS "In the Beginning." my timeline perceptions all start with the created Cross on the Donkey's back; then waited until He could scribe His Word during the papyrus era, then scribed were the words of prophecy of His intent to come visit His Creation. Recall that the word "Bible" is a Greek word for the papyrus plant and a useful timeline factor. Our Creator came among us as His Son Jesus; then spent a little over 30 earth years with us, eventually explaining Our Creator's desired Fatherly relationship with His Creation, or His Earth Family. He accepted and knew full well that He could not return to His Spiritual Abode as an old man like me.

If Jesus had passed away from old age, His name and efforts, or works, would probably be forgotten within a generation or two. He knew that for Our Creator Father to be Honored by "all" His kids and feel welcome to seek His offered Spiritual Heaven Home, that He would need to first reach and honor the least of thee, past, present and future; that their imperfections would never be a factor during or after this prophesized visit. John 19:30.

For His tailored visit with His mankind creation to be successful, Jesus and His Gospel messages would need to be first credible and accepted. To me, the Old Testament reeks with fear or negative overtones. Apparently, Our Creator Daddy thought so as well, and gave His Son Jesus, the full authority to flavor His Gospel messages with Positives such as, Faith, Hope, Trust and above all, Love. His tailored visit even included a subtle demo of His How and His Means of His personal return or resurrection back to His Creator Father: Sir Jesus was thereby summoned to the sickness and death situation of Lazarus, and Jesus stated in John 11:4 that "this sickness is not unto death, but for the glory of God, that the Son of God might be glorified thereby." Sir Jesus did raise Lazarus from the tomb and Siri stated that this was Jesus' last miracle prior to His own preplanned resurrection back to His Creator Father. Jesus said, Father, I thank you that you have heard me. I knew that you always hear me, but I said this on account of the people standing around, that they may believe that you sent me." John 11:41-44.

The How and the Means of both these situations is totally in concert with Our Creator's Spiritual Energy Domain, and His instant capability to respond to

His Son's Positive prayer request with a Positive Spiritual Energy booster, as in Lazarus' situation. As previously written above, I personally witnessed this capability in response to my Faith back in 2011, and I would presume that Jesus' requested Prayer for a Spiritual Energy booster would replicate a modern-day defibrillator. And for Jesus Himself, the situation necessity to openly prove and show the Positive Power of Prayer with Our Creator Father and that Our Creator Daddy is listening 24/7. Plus, His efforts and endeavors to Honor Our Creator were on the line. So vitally important, His personal Divinity would need to be forever credible and remembered as well to stand the test of time. Thus, a savvy leader of all mankind must first be a servant; thus, so symbolized and recorded within His Gospels when Jesus washed the feet of His disciples. John 13:14-15. So, Our Creator preplanned the most demeaning, the most humbling theater execution of the era; plus, cruelly memorable. Then using Judas, who triggered in "my Opinion," a "preplanned, already scripted," a never-to-be forgotten, middle-earth age return of His Son Jesus to His/Our Creator Father's right hand. THEN LEAVING BEHIND ANOTHER, NEVER-TO-BE FORGOTTEN IMAGE, the CROSS, a perfect matching visual image to the CROSS on back of Our Creator Father's Humble Servant, The Donkey.

So, Ladies and Gentlemen, of thee living earthly jury, I contend that thee clear and simple visible evidence, does clearly and truly authenticate Our Creator Father as "thee" only Entity that "could write or would write" His incredible manuscript; then signed and notarize His Word with His hallmark symbol, albeit humble, thee forever Royal CROSS!!!

In so doing, does truly authenticate with the Cross and its implication that any belief in the Cross, will grant all believers eternal life and return all believers back to Our Creator Father, using the very same Spiritual Energy that created all that "IS" during Our Creator's

"IN HIS BEGINNING!"

And if that is not enough, consider that Our Creator's Word informed mankind back in Genesis, that He used a rib from a man to create a woman. Probably irrelevant to some, but that timeline recorded fact, probably was not taken seriously, or noticed until our Xray capability came along. Until then, probably accepted as an authored allegory. I think this farm boy used that broad-use word correctly. Did anyone notice that I did not capitalize the word "my," when at the beginning of a sentence throughout this book. This book was written to "Exalt" Our Creator, and not me, or accepted writing mechanics. And surely noted throughout this book of my Blessings and lifetime perceptions, that I just love run-on sentences, or as I call them, excited writing!!! College English Composition teachers just did not understand my excited love for life, I guess. I think I will give them the benefit of doubt, as they were probably telling me that my big fat "F" was for "Fine try, Farm boy!"

In college, I lived on CliffsNotes, or like starting first grade reading all over again: See Our Creator create, see Baby Jesus in a manger, see a Donkey standing nearby, see Jesus speak the Gospels, see Jesus walk on water, see Jesus ride His Donkey into Jerusalem, see Jesus represent all of Our Creator Daddy's kids upon the Cross!!! Amen!!! Yup, just a quick read to recall just the essentials. So summarily, in "my Opinion," Our Creator Daddy does everything in His Universe with the very same Energy that He used "In His Beginning;" thus, facilitating an Energy Pathway back to Our Creator Daddy. Genesis stated that His kids were created "In His Image," or in "my Opinion," that Our Creator Daddy is "Spiritually wired" to His kids via "our inner 'small' voice." And that Our Creator Daddy becomes able to connect His Spiritual Energy to our body internal electrical circuitry by His creation design of mankind. Earthly scholars and scientists call that our body circuitry, or our neural system. Siri has all the details for all those readers who wish to connect more dots from our "inner 'small' voice" back to Our Creator Daddy via "In His Image" network. Siri says that our body network is comprised of innumerable atoms and around 60 essential elements, where several are listed on the back of a vitamin bottle, or found in the earth that we walk on. And our bodies take on electrical conductivity through our body atoms, which are comprised of Protons and are Positive charged, also electrons or negatives and neutrons. In my Opinion, Our Creator Daddy monitors our Protons 24/7 and responds to all Positive requests during our lifetime and/or our split-second needs when necessary. Also read Our Creator's Word, of course and a book on electricity; then, note the symbiotic relationship within our Universe. Like "spirit," electricity is also invisible, but that "energy" is definitely ongoing within our midst!!! Yup, Our Creator Daddy is always available!!! In His Word, Our Creator Daddy called His first kids Adam and Eve, but maybe they were family familiar names and that their birth names were actually Atom and Evolution. Yup, just stirring the thinking pot!!!

I often feel that I could write forever about Honoring Our Creator, and to thank Him for all my Blessings, but "two" words is all that I need to hear to please me, or remind me how Blessed I am: Dad and Grampa, and I am totally sure that Our Creator Common Daddy feels exactly the same!!! So, everyone, this book has a dual purpose, first my Matthew 28 commission to Honor Our Creator and His Son Jesus; then merged and equally important, with Grampa's life diary-like storyline, or a heritage backstory for the benefit of my Grandchildren.

I presume that I am allowed to use the word "benediction," and that my closing prayer wishes for my family, friends and all readers, or simply all Our Creator's Church, or all His people around His World, is that all would "first" find their first fortune in Blessings. And that all their copper pennies, whether lost like mine or not, turn into Golden memories like mine. These are the true "pennies from Heaven!!!" Amen!!!

Soon, I will turn eighty as this book is published, and when I do finally grow up, I would like to be like my Grandkids' Daddy, my eldest Son—Perfect from birth!!! And so important to publish before the world, that I am eternally grateful to his also Perfect life-mate, or Our Creator's creation, His Demigoddess "Mom" for my Grandchildren. One should always keep in mind that Grandchildren reflect, sweeten our lives, and are a zillion-to-one genetically. Grandchildren truly do make one's life Complete!!!

As we Honor Our Creator, and if my readers noted any occasional humor, just remember where that came from!!! Answer: Yup, you are right, from our Daddy's "Own" Image, Genesis 1:27!!! What a "cool" Common Daddy!!! And of course, check out the Donkeys!!! They do "carry" Our Creator's Notary Stamp with them at all times!!!

I mentioned above that I would soon be turning eighty, well it's April 2021 and this is the month. And it's also Easter and my Mom's same-day birthday; with my Dad's birthday in late April as well. I am so appreciative of their teachings that led to my youthful respect for Our Creator and His Risen Son, Sir Jesus. Within Our Creator's Word, we find our individual commission to spread His Risen Son's Gospels from one to another, and this book was written as a memoir to honor that commissioned endeavor. Please note that there is only one verse in Our Creator's Word that scares me: That verse is Matthew 10:33, so check it out!!!

I am eternally grateful for all my life affiliations, encounters and wisdoms that presented me insight as to How Our Creator does His thing throughout His Universe and beyond. But here on mother earth, I am grateful for my simple grasp of the difference and the relevance of the X or the valid contractual symbol, the + or the Positive electrical energy symbol, and the Cross; all with two crossing lines. My "Wrap" opinion is that Our Creator's "Wrap" Signature Symbol is the Cross that Our Creator Daddy intentionally scribed on the back of His intended servant, the Donkey, during His "In The Beginning," and intended to become His authenticating symbol. For Our Creator's Son, Jesus, the "Empty Cross" was His "Wrap" Scene, and for my book as well.

"The greatest legacy one can pass on
to one's children and grandchildren is
a legacy of character and faith."

—Billy Graham

"Honor Our Creator with Bold Aspirations
and a little-guts, this combo gritty attitude
goes a long way in helping Our Creator
Daddy bestow His Blessings."

—Grampa

By: Grampa Link Thompson

Milton Keynes UK
Ingram Content Group UK Ltd.
UKHW010845211223
434780UK00001B/64